THE 10 COIN COMMANDMENTS

Change Your Mind, Change Your Money

Bahir Jessie
Newark, New Jersey

https://10coincommandments.com

ISBN: 979-8-218-89445-0

Printed in the United States of America

Library of Congress Control Number: 2025921172

First Edition: October 2025

Contents

BeReshit (תִּישָׁאֶרְב)

*"In the beginning God created
the heaven and the earth." – Genesis 1:1*

THE *10 COIN COMMANDMENTS BIBLICAL FINANCIAL SYSTEM* originates from replicating YHWH (הוהי) in the creation of all things. As we are made in His image, the image of divine creation, the Holy Spirit provides layered revelations through the same Bible verse. This verse offers profound guidance on how God's wisdom enables you to achieve your financial goals. Revelations from the first verse of the Bible inspired me to create the *10 Coin Commandments Biblical Financial System*. Those revelations inspired me to refocus on God, the source of financial transformation.

BeReshit means in the beginning, at the origin, or at the start. The first verse in Genesis 1:1 represents three trinities within one. The first trinity introduced is time, which represents the past, the present, and the future. Time is the first construct that binds everything in this realm.

The second trinity, heaven, represents length, width, and height. Some would reject the idea that heaven has the physical limitations of a three-dimensional object. However, if heaven is considered in the physical realm instead of the spiritual realm, where there are no dimensional limitations, it encompasses distance in miles (length), depth (width), and finally height, representing that which is above.

The final trinity is the earth, which represents solid, liquid, and gas.

In the beginning, or within *time* (past, present, and future), God *created* the *heaven* (length, width, and height) and the *earth* (solid, liquid, and gas).

The first verse describes God as the creator, and we exercise our likeness, being made in the image of God, when we create. The key is to create like God using the formula for creation. Therefore, in creating the *10 Coin Commandments Biblical Financial System*, I've used the formula to create a process to help you achieve financial success. I used the following thirteen revelations to create this financial system.

Wisdom & Prayer

"The LORD by wisdom hath founded (created) the earth; by understanding hath he established (created) the heavens. By his knowledge the depths are broken up (separation of firmament, heaven, and earth), and the clouds (gas and liquid) drop down the dew (liquid)." – Proverbs 3:19-20

"In **wisdom** God created the heaven and the earth." Before you can begin to do anything, you need the requisite wisdom.

Imagine asking your two-month-old child to grab the groceries from the car. The child is neither physically strong enough nor sufficiently developed to understand the instructions, know what is required to accomplish the task, or comprehend the potential risks. The child does not have the tools needed to accomplish the goal. It would be the parents' fault for even asking with the expectation that the young child could comprehend the request. You need to take the same approach to your finances. Do not begin a financial activity without the correct knowledge.

What if you don't have the wisdom to create financial goals? You can take comfort in knowing that the wisdom actually does exist. True, the level of financial maturity and sophistication depends on the individual, as we all have different financial goals. However, no matter your financial goals or your current financial circumstance, there exists the wisdom to achieve your financial goals under God's purpose and authority. Spend the effort to find the wisdom you need. The best way to gain access to God's infinite financial wisdom is through **prayer.**

Time

Every financial instrument has time attached to it. There are times when industries, markets, and economies perform more favorably. All debt instruments have maturity dates. Understanding time within finance is very important. Time within finance can provide flexibility or be restrictive. The time you enter into a market or financial instrument determines the potential profit or loss. Similarly, the time you decide to exit a financial instrument will determine your cost, along with the potential profit or loss in a given transaction.

The time value of money is an important concept, as the buying power of a dollar is greater today than it is tomorrow due to inflation. As a result, the dollars you have today need to be invested in order to generate interest (capital gains) to outpace inflation. The future value of money determines what the money you receive today is worth in the future if you invest it. Therefore, time is an important factor when making financial decisions.

Motion

"In **motion**, transit, or movement, God created the heaven and the earth." The world is in constant motion, from the Earth revolving around the sun to people always on the go. If you're not moving, you're dying. This is why businesses are always referred to as a "going concern" in the world of finance. It's also why growth strategies are vital to the life of the business. The business must continue to grow. As an individual, you must grow every day. Growth requires motion.

Perspective

"With **perspective,** through **omnipresence,** God (The All Knowing) created the heaven and the earth." God is omnipresent. Therefore, God has every perspective and vantage point. This is why when God gives instructions, it's so difficult to fully understand. We need to just trust God. We don't realize that God is always in the perfect position, which is every position, and can see every outcome. God, having every vantage point, can provide the perfect instruction because He has the perfect perspective.

We are unable to understand what God sees because we are not in the same position. God has the complete perspective. This is why it is important to lean on God's perspective when creating your financial plan. It is also important to get perspectives from your trusted advisors regarding certain financial decisions.

Objectivity

"In **objectivity** God created the heaven and the earth." Perspective can help provide objectivity. However, objectivity is the quality or character of having a lack of favoritism toward one side or another, where there is freedom from bias. As you think about your financial decisions, you will need to reflect on whether there is any bias. Is your financial plan objective? Is your business plan free of bias? Lack of objectivity is harmful to your financial well-being. By removing your emotions, you will be able to make sound financial decisions. Now, every decision we make has some emotion involved because we're human. However, objectivity protects you from allowing your emotions to cause you to make poor financial decisions, especially those that may hurt others.

Order

"In **order** God created the heaven and the earth." God's creation and actions demonstrate a preference for order, logic, and harmony. *"For God is not the author of confusion, but of peace, as in all churches of the saints." – 1 Corinthians 14:33 "Let all things be done decently and in order." – 1 Corinthians 14:40*

We need to keep our financial house in order. Within the structured and organized example of divine creation, financial order provides clarity, control, stability, security, improved decision-making, autonomy, and empowerment. Order is the necessary structure by which God allows you to operate to receive financial blessings. God's financial order is logical and harmonious. Financial order prevents financial conflicts with your spouse, family, and the community. A sound structure for personal, family, business, and community finance with God at the forefront requires order.

Truth

"In **truth** God created the heaven and the earth." If you have the complete perspective and are objective—absent of bias— you are living in truth. *"Jesus saith unto him, I am the way, the truth, and the life: no man cometh unto the Father, but by me."* – John 14:6

Financial truth requires discernment. Understanding how to properly use your talents to maximize earnings requires an honest evaluation that will sometimes show some deficiencies with room for improvement. Knowing the right type of people to surround yourself with to grow future earning potential requires an honest and truthful look at everyone with whom you are associated. The ability to determine whether you are helping yourself achieve financial success or recognizing bad financial habits that impede your progress requires truth. This high level of transparency builds consistency, allows you to make informed decisions, and increases financial engagement. Be desperate for the financial truth to gain the perspective that will provide deliverance. The financial truth is a healing process that will make you better.

As the tree of life, which is the pathway to God, would explain, "In wisdom, time, motion, perspective, objectivity, order, prayer, and truth God created the heaven and the earth." Likewise, in wisdom, time, motion, perspective, objectivity, order, prayer, and truth, you will earn income, create a business, buy real estate, invest, and achieve your financial goals.

"O Timothy, keep that which is committed to thy trust, avoiding profane and vain babblings, and oppositions of science falsely so called: Which some professing have erred concerning the faith. Grace be with thee. Amen." – 1 Timothy 6:20

God warns against pseudo-science, or false knowledge, that pulls you away from the truth. This is not a condemnation of science. Science is one of the ways in which God communicates and shares His brilliance and wisdom. However, false and misleading statements that masquerade as science to mislead are in opposition to God, who is truth. Make sure the Holy Spirit is guiding you along the way.

Faith

*"Through **faith** we understand that the worlds were framed by the **word** of God, so that things which are seen were not made of things which do appear." – Hebrews 11:3*

*"By **faith** Enoch was translated that he should not see death; and was not found, because God had translated him: for before his translation he had this testimony, that he pleased God. But without faith it is impossible to please him: for he that cometh to God must believe that he is, and that he is a rewarder of them that diligently seek him." – Hebrews 11:5-6*

Faith is what activates God's covering and blessings. God knowing that you trust him is the only way. Let me warn you! Faith today is not faith tomorrow. Many have not received what God promised because they lost faith along the way. On the journey to financial freedom, there will be circumstances that test your faith. At some point in your journey, you will find yourself in situations leading you to believe you are going to lose your house, savings, friends, and all that you've worked very hard for. It's going to take faith to keep going. Everything around you will appear to be falling apart. Focus on passing the test and not the chaos the test brings. Speak to God every morning, throughout the day, and at night. Faith in God is manifested through prayer, studying scripture, seeking God's wisdom, praise, thankfulness, and giving God your undivided priority and attention. Trust God to bring you through!

Discipline

Success in finance over time requires **discipline**. This level of financial discipline is more science than it is art. Some of the folklore of how people have obtained riches never speaks to the methodical, disciplined approach. Financial discipline requires consistency in good behaviors that will allow you to make informed decisions to achieve your financial goals. Financial discipline using the *10 Coin Commandments Biblical Financial System* includes budgeting, saving, debt management, avoiding unnecessary spending, and adhering to a plan for long-term financial stability. Financial discipline may be difficult in the beginning, but it's necessary for executing the financial plan. Building good habits, increasing focus, applying self-control, and allocating time for ongoing financial education will require discipline.

Location & Position

In the beginning God created the earth. The continent of Africa was called by His children (original inhabitants) ALKEBU-LAN, EL BILAD AL SUDAN (WEST AFRICAN JEWISH COMMUNITIES), EDEN, CUSH, and KEMET.

The continent was renamed Africa, but the original name, Alkebu-Lan, is the oldest and most indigenous, which means "Mother of Mankind" or "Eden". This name for the continent was used by the Moors, Nubians, Khart-Haddans (Carthagenians), and Cushites (Ethiopians). The current name Africa is an inaccurately translated term adopted by most today.

The name Africa was given to the continent by ancient Romans. Other names that refer to Africa are Kemet, Libya, Ortegia, Corphye, Olympia, Hesperia, Oceania, and Ta-Merry.

"And the LORD God planted a garden eastward in Eden; and there he put the man whom he had formed. And out of the ground made the LORD God to grow every tree that is pleasant to the sight, and good for food; the tree of life also in the midst of the garden, and the tree of knowledge of good and evil. And a river went out of Eden to water the garden; and from thence it was parted, and became into four heads. The name of the first is Pison: that is it which compasseth the whole land of Havilah (Arabia), where there is gold; And the gold of that land is good: there is bdellium and the onyx stone. And the name of the second river is Gihon: the same is it that compasseth the whole land of Ethiopia (Cush). And the name of the third river is Hiddekel (Tigris river, Sumeria, Babylon, Iran, Turkey, North Mesopotamia): that is it which goeth toward the east of Assyria. And the fourth river is Euphrates (Ancient Mesopotamia, Persian Gulf, Iraq, Syria, Turkey)." – Genesis 2:8-14

The Bible outlines the lineage of African nations in order. *"And the sons of Ham; Cush (Ethiopia), and Mizraim (Egypt), and Phut (Libya), and Caanan (Israel, Palestine, Lebanon). And the sons of Cush; Seba (Sudan), and Havilah (Arabia), and Sabtah (Southern Coast of Arabia), and Raamah (Oman, United Arab Emirates), and Sabtecha (Somalia): and the sons of Raamah; Sheba (Yemen), and Dedan (Saudi Arabia). And Cush begat Nimrod: he began to be a mighty one in the earth. He was a mighty hunter before the LORD: wherefore it is said, Even as Nimrod the mighty hunter before the LORD. And the beginning of his kingdom was Babel (Babylon), and Erech (Southeastern Iraq), and Accad (Northern Mesopotamia, Bagdad), and*

Calneh (Northern Iraq), in the land of Shinar (Mesopotamia)."
– Genesis 10:6-10

Many have been misled to believe that Havilah (Arabia), Cush (Ethiopia), Assyria (Mesopotamia), Persia, and Syria were separated and disconnected. In biblical times, they were very much connected as the Nile flowed from southern Ethiopia and emptied into the Great Sea (Mediterranean), where people from lower Africa journeyed to Northeast Africa (Canaan, Palestine or Israel). Only in the 19th century, during the era of World War II, was Northeast Africa referred to as the "Middle East" in an attempt to erase its African lineage. Yet, hundreds of ancient Shrines of the Black Madonna have existed in many parts of North Africa, Europe, and Russia. The oldest Bibles have pictures of Moses, Christ, Mary, and the Apostles as what we would call Nubians, Black people, or those of African descent.

"After this I looked, and, behold, a door was opened in heaven: and the first voice which I heard was as it were of a trumpet talking with me; which said, Come up hither, and I will shew thee things which must be hereafter. And immediately I was in the spirit; and, behold, a throne was set in heaven, and one sat on the throne. And he that sat was to look upon like a jasper and a sardine stone: and there was a rainbow round about the throne, in sight like unto an emerald." – Revelations 4:1-3

The oldest human was found in present-day Tanzania, which correlates to the Bible's account of the Garden of Eden in Genesis. Tanzania in biblical times would have been in southern Cush (Ethiopia). The Nile is usually associated with Egypt, though it in fact flows through 11 countries: Tanzania, Uganda, the Democratic Republic of Congo, Rwanda, Burundi, Ethiopia, Kenya, Eritrea, South Sudan, Sudan, and Egypt.

"And the LORD God planted a garden eastward in Eden; and there he put the man whom he had formed." – Genesis 2:8

"This is the book of the generations of Adam. In the day that God created man, in the likeness of God made he him; Male and female created he them; and blessed them, and called <u>their</u> name Adam, in the day when they were created." – Genesis 5:1-2

Eden translates to paradise, pleasure, or delight. In Genesis, God created a delightful, perfect **location** to put Adam. In the same way, God is creating the delightful, perfect place with everything you already need to be successful. Do not hold on to the old place, location, state of mind, or situation. God is making a new place with new resources, the right people, new capital, and a new environment. God will not change the old things to bless you with something new. God will require you to leave the old habits, bad environments, troubled people, job, or physical location and put you in a place he's created just for you. God created Eden before he put man there. In the same way, God has already created the perfect place for you to be successful with everything you need. Trust where God is taking you. Wherever God places you, remember it will be your job to dress it and to keep it, which means to take care of, preserve, protect, work, produce, grow, nourish, bear fruit, and be responsible for it.

The Law Giver

Ma'at represented attributes of God that embody the principles of law, order, justice, and balance. This was done through 42 negative confessions (commandments) which predate Moses by 2,000 years. Examples of the 42 negative confessions are: "I have not committed sin;" "I have not stolen;" "I have not slain man or woman;" "I have not uttered lies;" "I have not committed adultery;" "I have not debauched the wives of other men;" and "I have not false accused anyone".

Several financial principles can be taken from these 42 Negative Confessions, which include:

- "I have not stolen grain."
- "I have not stolen cultivated land."
- "I have not stopped the flow of water of a neighbor."

Grain was a key unit of value in ancient Egypt (Kemet) and essential for trade with other countries. The land in Egypt was very fertile, which produced an abundance of crops, including wheat, barley, flax, fruits, vegetables, papyrus, and spices. Grain was important to the operations of the government. In addition, cattle, or other livestock, were important to the barter system. Farmers would even pay taxes with cattle. Water is essential to crop growth and overall agricultural production. The laws of money, regarding fair and equitable uses within society, are reflected in these commandments.

"In which time Moses was born, and was exceeding fair, and nourished up in his father's house three months: And when he was cast out, Pharaoh's daughter took him up, and nourished him for her own son. And Moses was learned in all the wisdom of the Egyptians, and was mighty in words and in deeds."
– Acts 7:20-22

The concept of gods

The ancient African religion has traditions and concepts that were passed down over a millennium, which have been misinterpreted, or are flat-out lies, for the purpose of miseducation. The lowercase god is a class of being, such as a human, plant or animal. The term is used to mean a powerful entity that is responsible for existence.

In ancient Kemet, the serpent represented wisdom. That being said, the serpent also represented fallen angels who gave man forbidden wisdom. *"Behold, I send you forth as sheep in the midst of wolves: be ye therefore wise as serpents, and harmless as doves." – Matthew 10:16*

When it comes to gods, humans in particular, there is the ability to create our own realities. God wanted to make it clear that He is the Creator, the One True God, the Was, Is, and Forever Will Be YHWH. Over time, some strayed and began worshiping gods in the manner they should only worship the LORD God. The Bible made it clear that such idolatry is a sin.

"And God spake all these words, saying, I am the LORD thy God, which have brought thee out of the land of Egypt, out of the house of bondage. Thou shalt have no other gods before me." – Exodus 20:1-3

"Neither be ye idolaters, as were some of them; as it is written, The people sat down to eat and drink, and rose up to play." – 1Corinthians 10:7

God must be the center of everything you do. Anything we acquire without God will require that we maintain it without

God. As a result, those things we've acquired without God add more distance, which eventually severs our relationship.

All that we acquire through God will require us to continue to seek His presence in our lives. People have taken up many idols. Money has become an idol for the current culture, where there is an absence of God. The *10 Coin Commandments Biblical Financial System* puts God at the center to strengthen your relationship with Him.

"No man can serve two masters: for either he will hate the one, and love the other; or else he will hold to the one, and despise the other. Ye cannot serve God and mammon (money)."
– Matthew 6:24

Through Christ

"In the beginning was the Word, and the Word was with God, and the Word was God. The same was in the beginning with God. All things were made by him; and without him was not any thing made that was made. In him was life; and the life was the light of men (Christ). And the light shineth in darkness; and the darkness comprehended it not. There was a man sent from God, whose name was John (Yohan). The same came for a witness, to bear witness of the Light (Christ), that all men through him might believe." – John 1:1-7

Christ was there in the beginning with God, and only through Christ can you gain access to the Father. The *10 Coin Commandment Biblical Financial System* teaches that through Christ, you can reach your full financial power, achieving all of your goals in every good work.

"Jesus answered them, Is it not written in your law, I said, Ye are gods? If he called them gods, unto whom the word of God came, and the scripture cannot be broken; Say ye of him, whom the Father hath sanctified, and sent into the world, Thou blasphemest; because I said, I am the Son of God? If I do not the works of my Father, believe me not. But if I do, though ye believe not me, believe the works: that ye may know, and believe, that the Father is in me, and I in him."
– John 10:34-38

Revelation

There is a call to return to God's divine order, especially regarding stewardship. The *10 Coin Commandments Biblical Financial System* reconnects you to God's divine wisdom. We have been operating in the world without the Holy Spirit and disconnected from God when it comes to money. This biblical financial system was created in the image of God so that you can foster a deep spiritual connection by building a relationship with God through Christ to achieve your financial goals.

Therefore, with wisdom, in time, in motion, with perspective, objectivity, order, prayer, truth, faith, discipline, at the perfect location, in the image of God, and through Christ, God created the heaven and the earth.

Likewise, with wisdom, in time, in motion, with perspective, objectivity, order, prayer, truth, faith, discipline, at the perfect location, in the image of God, and through Christ, you will create multiple streams of income, start businesses, buy real estate, invest, and achieve your financial dreams, doing every good work.

Introduction

CONVERSATIONS ABOUT MONEY, investing, and saving can be intimidating. Money is vital to achieving your dreams of owning your own business, finding alternative ways to create income, planning for retirement, protecting your assets, setting aside money for an emergency, providing a quality education for you and your family, and wealth creation. Typically, discussions involving your personal finances are completely separate from God. However, God should be at the center of everything, especially when it comes to money.

At fifteen, as a high school sophomore, I began writing down Bible verses about money. In studying the Word, I saw how God's instructions generated supernatural results. I've seen what happens when we try to manage our money without God's presence and wisdom. I've also experienced the transformation that occurs when we align our financial decisions with God's Word. As a Business Banking Credit Analyst Manager, Wealth Management Private Banking Regional Credit Manager, and Private Equity Credit Officer, I've worked with companies, individuals, and families to help them achieve financial success. The *10 Coin Commandments Biblical Financial System* is designed to meet you wherever you are, no matter your level of financial sophistication.

The *10 Coin Commandments Financial System* is a biblical roadmap for reclaiming control over your finances. The system provides instructions using biblical principles to help you achieve all of your financial goals. This financial framework changes how you think about money. In changing how you think about money, you will begin to actively change your financial situation.

No one is without financial stress. Most people feel overwhelmed when it comes to making decisions about money, not because they are lazy, but because of the lack of information and access to a better way.

Money is only a tool. It requires the acceptance of a system of shared assumptions, values, and beliefs that govern how you behave concerning its use. Those who do not understand how money works are susceptible to a cycle of dysfunction, subjecting themselves to financial bondage. Biblical principles will help guide you through every financial decision.

Approximately 77% of adults report that their stress about their personal finances has either remained the same or gotten worse, according to the Mind over Money survey by Capital One and the Decision Lab. Concerns about money include a lack of savings, growing health care costs, student loan debt, retirement, low wages, lifestyle costs, taxes, limited access to credit or capital, inflation, and lack of an emergency fund. Shockingly, the constant fear and stress associated with personal finances happen to everyone regardless of their socio-economic status.

Truthfully, the more money you have, the harder you need to work to properly manage it. Articles published on the Nasdaq website report that seventy percent of generational wealth is lost after the second generation. Ninety percent of generational wealth is lost after the third generation. The *10 Coin Commandments Biblical Financial System* is easy to follow, can be applied to the most complicated circumstances, and has the flexibility to expand or contract to fit your specific financial needs.

The system shifts the focus beyond the idea of getting rich. The purpose is to put God at the center of your life and your finances. The financial transformation does not allow you to hide or overlook past mistakes. You don't know who you truly are until you understand how, when, why, and where you use money. Money is a behavioral science. Therefore, you can't properly manage your money without understanding your behavior. The *10 Coin Commandments Biblical Financial System* is based on scripture; there is no greater way to build a relationship with God and get the necessary financial instruction provided by the LORD.

"But continue thou in the things which thou hast learned and hast been assured of, knowing of whom thou hast learned them; And that from a child thou hast known the holy scriptures, which are able to make thee wise unto salvation through faith which is in Christ Jesus." – 2 Timothy 3:14-15

"All scripture is given by inspiration of God, and is profitable for doctrine, for reproof, for correction, for instruction in

righteousness: That the man of God may be perfect, thoroughly furnished unto all good works." – 2 Timothy 3:16-17

To overcome the triggers of financial stress, begin by confronting your fears, assigning a clear purpose to your income, and creating a strategic plan to increase your earning potential. Without purpose, money–like people–falls by the wayside.

Most people believe that parents are responsible for teaching their kids about money. Taking the time to discuss money with your children through creative storytelling and life experiences increases their chances of making sound financial decisions as adults. The system I've created addresses how to pass biblical financial principles to the next generation while creating a framework of accountability for yourself.

This is about breaking generational cycles of lack, isolation, shame, and abuse. It's about refusing to let misinformation, bad habits, and a disconnection from God keep you in financial bondage.

The *10 Coin Commandments* will help you:

- Assign a clear purpose to every dollar you earn
- Build sustainable habits grounded in scripture
- Discern and resist financial traps that prey on the uninformed
- Reframe your relationship with money centered on the Word and exercised through faith

"Envy thou not the oppressor, and choose none of his ways. For the froward is abomination to the LORD: but his secret is with the righteous." – Proverbs 3:31-32

Those in positions of influence who justify poor spiritual, personal, and financial choices—elevating their own judgment above righteousness—act in direct contradiction to God's Word. Do not follow them. In a money-obsessed culture, idolizing people with terrible character because you covet their wealth is a significant misstep grounded in personal lusts. God warns against following the oppressor, who likely exhibits personality traits of Machiavellianism, narcissism, sociopathy, and psychopathy. The scripture teaches how to identify the danger (spiritual, financial, or physical), protect yourself, and navigate your way through the wilderness to abundance.

Having control over material resources gives you a significant advantage in the pursuit of financial freedom. Often, inefficiencies in the system—whether natural or intentionally created—present unique opportunities to build wealth. Understanding how money is made in these moments not only helps you protect what you already have but also puts you in a stronger position to seize future opportunities.

"And God is able to make all grace abound toward you; that ye, always having all sufficiency in all things, may abound to every good work:" – 2 Corinthians 9:8

We are saved by grace—God's unearned and undeserved favor. It is not through our own efforts or justification, but through His grace alone, that we are provided with all we need. To abound means to have abundance—more than enough. Through His abundant grace, God equips us with everything required to carry out every good work. He responds to those with whom He has a relationship, and our obedience to His Word opens the door to His overflowing provision. That abundance includes wisdom, guidance, resources, protection, peace, and prosperity;

everything needed to fulfill our purpose and do good in the world.

Submission and obedience are important parts of this process. In my early twenties, I purchased a nice car. I was enjoying what success I was able to obtain at that time. I recall visiting the gas station and playing the lottery. God told me, "Your blessings come directly from me; not from games of chance." Understand that I had asked God to provide me with this nice car, and He did just that. So, I said, "Ok, I won't play the lottery anymore."

A few months passed, and the lottery jackpot had risen to a few hundred million. I stopped by the gas station to play the lottery after God warned me not to. I got a few tickets and walked to the car. It wouldn't start. I prayed and asked for forgiveness. It started.

You'll never guess what happened a few months later! I played it again. The lottery jackpot was over $1 billion. I was risking favor. I played the lottery and didn't win. This time, my car wouldn't start, and there was nothing I could say to God that would get me back in his favor. My continued disobedience came at a cost. The car was towed to the dealership, and I spent thousands of dollars to get it fixed. I haven't had any trouble since then. I learned my lesson.

This wasn't a coincidence. It was a correction. God was protecting me from a future without his covering. I needed to understand that his favor requires my obedience.

In the chapters ahead, we'll explore what the Bible says about money and techniques on how to apply scripture in everyday, practical ways. The system is built to get your financial house in order and accelerate your financial transformation.

We begin with prayer! I invite you to release everything that's weighing you down until now. Free yourself. Remove the shame. Eliminate the confusion. Eradicate financial double-mindedness and bad financial habits. Let's lay all of our financial burdens down and ask God for a fresh start.

Prayer of Deliverance

*Heavenly Father, I repent of any sins in my
life or my ancestors' lives that resulted in
a curse due to disobedience. I repent of all
disobedience, rebellion, perversion, witchcraft,
idolatry, lust, adultery, fornication, mistreatment
of others, murder, cheating, lying, sorcery,
divination and occult involvement, and ask for
Your Forgiveness and cleansing through the
blood of Jesus Christ.*

*I take authority over and break any and every
curse upon my life in the name of Jesus. I break
all curses of poverty, lack, debt, overspending,
spending more than I've earned, destruction,
sickness, death and vagabond. I break all curses
on my finances, marriage, family, children and
relationships. I break curses of rejection, pride,
rebellion, lust, hurt, incest, rape, Ahab, Jezebel,
fear, insanity, madness and confusion.*

*I break all curses affecting my finances,
mind, sexual character, emotions,
will and relationships.*

*I break every hex, jinx, spell,
and spoken curse over my life.*

*I break every fetter, shackle, chain, cord, habit,
and cycle that is the result of a curse.*

According to Galatians 3:13, I have been redeemed of the curse of the law by the sacrifice of Jesus. I exercise my faith in the blood of Jesus and loose myself and my descendants from any and every curse. I claim forgiveness through the blood of Jesus for the sins of the fathers.

All of my sins have been remitted and I loose myself from the curse that comes as a result of all disobedience and rebellion to the Word of God.

I exercise my faith, and I know that confession is made unto salvation (Romans 10:9-13). Therefore, I can confess that Abraham's blessings are mine. I am not cursed, but blessed. I am the head and not the tail. I am above and not beneath. I am blessed coming in and blessed going out. I am blessed, and what God has blessed cannot be cursed.

I command spirits of rejection, hurt, bitterness, unforgiveness, bondage, torment, death, destruction, fear, lust, perversion, mind control, witchcraft, poverty, lack, debt, confusion, double-mindedness, sickness, infirmity, pain, divorce, separation, strife, contention, depression, sadness, loneliness, self-pity, self-destruction, self-rejection, anger, rage, wrath, anguish, vagabond, greed, gluttony, pride, selfishness, envy, slothfulness, abuse and addiction to Come Out in the name of Jesus!

Lord, I thank you for setting me free from every curse and every spirit that has operated in my life. Amen.

Commandment I
Wisdom and Instruction

"To know wisdom and instruction;
to perceive the words of understanding;
To receive the instruction of wisdom,
justice, and judgement, and equity;
To give subtlety to the simple, to the
young man knowledge and discretion.
A wise man will hear, and will increase
learning; and a man of understanding
shall attain unto wise counsels:
To understand a proverb, and the interpretation;
the words of the wise, and their dark sayings."
– Proverbs 1:2-6

I T IS NEARLY IMPOSSIBLE TO BE SUCCESSFUL in anything without having the requisite information, understanding, wisdom and instruction. The key to gaining financial freedom is to be consistent in the pursuit of learning how to acquire, invest, and use money. In the same way that there are laws of the universe, laws of physics, and laws of mathematics, there are also laws of money. Learning those laws—and applying them consistently—is the foundation of financial freedom.

My formal banking and credit training experience spans over 20 years. No matter the level of financial sophistication of any one particular client, sound, accurate, and timely quality information is required to make good financial decisions.

THE FOUNDATION OF WISDOM

The Proverbs verse outlines the importance of wisdom and instruction, and the Bible highlights a three-step process in acquiring wisdom.

1. **Humility.** *"The fear of the LORD is the beginning of knowledge: but fools despise wisdom and instruction."* – *Proverbs 1:7* **The first part of the process** is humbling yourself to be able to receive the instruction and digest the information. In order to humble yourself to gain wisdom, you need submission to God.

To benefit from teaching, you must also have reverence for the wisdom and instruction you receive and respect for the teacher! It is foolish to be unreceptive to people who can impart wisdom. It is also foolish not to put forth the effort needed to acquire it.

Have you ever tried to teach someone who refused to accept the information? Or explained how to do something just to have them say, "I know" when they clearly didn't?

I remember trying to teach my eight-year-old twin cousins how to properly shoot a basketball. One of them listened. The other was proud and said, "I know." He had no idea. There was no humility; therefore, he was unable to receive the lesson and become better.

If you do not trust the financial information or the person providing the instruction, you need to verify the information, the instruction, and the teacher. The transfer of wisdom requires trust.

2. **Understanding.** After you've humbled yourself, the next step is to truly comprehend and apply what you've learned. After all, the benefits of wisdom and instruction are useless if you're unable to comprehend the information.

   Assess the financial information you've gained and lessons learned from the person providing it. Familiarize yourself with financial terms and definitions so that you're able to better digest the wisdom and instructions.

3. **Intent.** The Bible defines wisdom and instruction as something that provides justice, good judgment, and equity (impartiality). Therefore, wisdom and instruction must at all times be fair and impartial.

   Through this step in the process, we ensure, through our intent, that our wisdom leads to justice, good judgment and fairness. We also need to ensure that we are imparting our wisdom in the right way. To "give subtlety to the simple" means to provide wisdom in a delicate manner. How you provide wisdom and instruction is just as important as the instruction itself. "To the simple" means to provide wisdom and instruction to the innocent or those lacking wisdom.

   To ensure you are operating with the right intent once you receive financial wisdom, it's important to assess both the financial information and the person providing it. Be sure that the financial wisdom is just, not purposely designed to hurt or disenfranchise any individual or specific group. Verify that the financial wisdom exercises prudent judgment. Only implement financial wisdom that is safe, impartial, and unbiased.

Applying these principles on the quest to obtain financial wisdom is vital before developing a financial plan. These three principles—humility, understanding, and intent—are the foundation of financial wisdom. Before you can build a financial plan, you need this foundation in place. Think of it like building a house: no one starts with the roof or the walls before laying a solid foundation. If you've ever seen a rushed construction job, you know the long-term costs of poor craftsmanship. The same is true in your finances. Take the time to humble yourself, learn with understanding, and apply wisdom with the right intent. Doing this upfront gives you the blueprint and stability you need to make sound financial decisions that will last.

THE PERSONAL FINANCIAL AUDIT

It's important to understand that you are exactly the when, where, what, why, and how you spend money. Perform an internal audit to fully understand yourself, your household, and your family's decisions regarding the following:

- How do you make, spend, save, and invest money?
- When do you make, spend, save, and invest money?
- Where do you make, spend, save, and invest money?
- What do you make, spend, save, and invest money in?
- Why have you made those financial decisions?

A personal financial audit will help you identify financial health areas that must be improved. We sometimes make the mistake of assuming we know where improvement is needed without doing the work to identify the problem. The audit allows you to prioritize your financial goals once you realize where the weaknesses are.

The lessons in *The 10 Coin Commandments Biblical Financial System* will help you begin to understand the areas of your financial life that need improvement and provide guidance on how to improve them. Visit https://10coincommandments.com to download your free digital workbook for a guided personal financial audit exercise.

LOOKING FOR LOVE

Why you spend money is just as important as the how, when, what, and where in making wise financial decisions. Before any purchase, always ask yourself, "Why am I spending this money?" Income wasted masking insecurities from your past through the purchase of clothing and accessories like shoes, sneakers, jewelry, and luxury handbags only to feel acceptance is an absolute waste of time and speaks to a greater issue. Remember, you are what you spend money on. Planning how you're going to spend money you haven't earned comes directly from the how to-be-poor handbook. However, planning how to save and invest is a behavior that improves your financial position and starts you down the path to creating wealth.

The average wealthy person does not flaunt their wealth by wearing the most expensive and trendy clothes, driving exotic cars, or wearing fine jewelry. People are accustomed to seeing their favorite rich entertainers, whose clothes and jewelry are sponsored by various brands to promote products, wearing the latest and most expensive items as influencers of a desirable lifestyle that will entice consumers to buy what they didn't even pay for. Even if these entertainers did pay for the fancy items, they use tax write-offs for clothing, jewelry, and cars as business expenses. If you're chasing that lifestyle, you will likely end up poor. The huge mortgage, expensive car loans, yacht loan, and monthly expenses that have you spending more than you earn will put you in financial ruin. On average, wealthy individuals are smart with their money, acquiring income-producing assets to create generational wealth. They may have nice things, but they are living well below their means.

Decide whether you want to look rich or be wealthy, as it's unlikely you can successfully do both. Most wealthy people either married into money, inherited money, exploited a unique God given talent, got really lucky, owned or led a successful business, or saved money over a long period of time by spending less than they make and investing wisely.

It's human nature to be tribal in feeling the need to be accepted by family, friends, peers, and the greater society. However, instead of researching the latest consumption trends for the purpose of spending to feel accepted, research where people are spending or investing to understand what products or services are in demand, so you can take advantage of opportunities to make money.

- Create a financial calendar and schedule time every day to read financial articles and search financial websites for commentary on an array of topics that interest you. Understand where interest rates are headed, the housing market, unemployment, technology and the state of both the US and global economy.

- Create a financial reading list and build a financial library. Research the various types of income-producing assets to determine what you are comfortable acquiring to generate passive income. Most banks have a designated website with financial literacy information. Learn the many different types of financial products and their purpose to add value and improve your level of financial sophistication.

- Search for financial content on social media. The algorithm will continue to send financial information based on the videos you've viewed and liked as a result. Bankrate reported that approximately 80% of young adults get financial advice from social media. The platform has zero barriers to accessing good financial information, so choose trusted and proven content from multiple sources. You'll be able to evaluate the information on social media by comparing it to the financial advice provided on official financial websites, books, and the financial literacy material provided by banks.

Reevaluate your spending habits and gather all pertinent information needed to make better financial decisions. Make yourself vulnerable and take an honest look in the mirror. Running from your finances by not addressing all of the many underlying issues is disastrous. You are your finances. Our finances are reflective of the decisions we make. It will take effort to first correct how you think about money. It will take even greater effort to change your behavior to become the version of yourself that will allow God to bless you. *"But seek ye first the kingdom of God, and his righteousness; and all these things shall be added unto you." – Matthew 6:33*

FINANCIAL FEARS

Anxiety surrounding the many challenges of earning a sustainable income, managing your financial obligations, and investing for the future can be very overwhelming, particularly given the daily bombardment of lifestyle comparisons from social media, radio, streaming, movies, or music. Purposeful financial miseducation and overconsumption propaganda may lead to excess spending, zero savings, high levels of debt, a marginal retirement plan, and a paycheck-to-paycheck financial cycle. No one wants to be in an ongoing financial crisis every month. However, in order to improve your personal financial condition, you must first address all of your issues. Escapism is not a solution. You must face your financial reality. After you've assessed where you need to improve, you can begin seeking the wisdom, instruction, and advice needed to change your current financial situation.

Fiscal paralysis, which occurs when you regularly ignore your finances due to fear, laziness, or ignorance, will result in you unwittingly spending more than you earn, creating poor habits, and costing you hundreds of thousands of dollars that could have been used for saving and investing. Constantly putting yourself at risk of credit card late fees, past due bills, bank overdraft fees, and poor spending decisions will have an adverse impact on your credit report, making debt and insurance even more expensive. Everyone, no matter their socioeconomic status, deals with money anxiety from time to time. However, the increased stress of not earning enough to make ends meet or achieve long-term financial goals may lead to physical health issues, mental health issues, and even personal relationship issues if you don't address your financial concerns.

To overcome your fear, figure out what you are afraid of and the reasons why. Perhaps there's a good reason. You may be deep in debt and don't want to see how bad of a situation you've gotten yourself into. Maybe your issue is less complicated; maybe you just aren't a numbers person and are intimidated by financial planning. Whatever the reasons, write down your fears and recognize that inactivity makes your financial condition worse. A sound, responsible plan and action is the only way to overcome each fear. Let's address a few common financial fears:

Overwhelming Medical Expenses

Medical bills are one of the leading causes of bankruptcy filings, and approximately 78% of those filing for bankruptcy due to health and medical issues had health insurance, per a study conducted by Harvard University. Many of us struggle with healthcare expenses despite supposedly having adequate healthcare insurance.

What if you need a drug that your current insurance carrier doesn't cover? What if your insurance provider doesn't cover the doctor most capable and experienced to treat your current condition? Depending on the medical procedure or health condition, the insurance company may not provide enough coverage, leaving you with significant medical expenses that put a strain on your finances.

Unfortunately, until this country joins the rest of the civilized world and considers health care a human right and not a commodity, this is the reality. So, your six-figure salary, job security, emergency fund, and retirement account may not make you immune to crippling medical expenses and medical debt.

One way to protect yourself from overwhelming medical bills is to purchase supplemental insurance in addition to your regular health coverage. If you receive a large bill, always request an itemized statement and check it carefully for errors. Insurance claims are often denied because of simple mistakes or outdated billing codes, so review the charges and ask your insurer to explain any non-covered items. If the bill is legitimate but not fully covered, contact the hospital or doctor to negotiate a long-term payment plan. In some cases, charities or assistance programs can also help offset the cost.

Market Collapse

It is important to know there is no reason to leave **all** of your money in a savings or checking account, which, if you're lucky, provides a return of 1.90% and doesn't outpace the average inflation rate of 2.8%. As a result, dollars in savings accounts are losing real-world value as the cost of goods and services continues to increase by an average of three percent while you earn less than two percent interest.

For many, investing is too complicated. The fear of the stock market is also based on the news reporting of doomsday scenarios, whether accurate or inaccurate. Capital (cash) constraints and preferential treatment to large clients (Hedge Funds, Private Equity Funds, Pension Funds, etc.) who deploy large amounts of cash and can negotiate lower commissions and fees, make it difficult for the average person to benefit from trading stock. Initial Public Offerings (IPO's) are reserved for preferred clients (Hedge Funds, Private Equity Funds, Pension Funds, Ultra-High Net Worth Individuals). The average investor won't get a chance to participate, nor will they have the opportunity to create significant wealth from these stocks.

For short-term investors, big losses happen more often as the stock market's volatility may move for a variety of reasons, from changes in the business cycle to new regulations or the current political climate. However, when employing long-term strategies, it is unlikely that you will lose big in the stock market. Generally, huge losses occur during short-term get-rich-quick strategies. It is important that your investments have a diverse mix of bonds, mutual funds, and stocks to mitigate those risks. If you want to create and grow wealth, passive income investing is the way to do it. If you want to lose money, letting it sit in a checking or savings account is a definite way to do it, as the savings will not outpace inflation.

It's important to have a checking and savings account to manage the inflow of income and outflow of expenses. However, after you've saved six to twelve months of your salary (which we'll dive into more), any excess money should be put to work.

Many prefer to invest in real estate and not the stock market to create wealth. This is an excellent strategy, but you must know what you're doing. The Foreign Exchange Market, also known as Forex, is where people trade different currencies— like dollars for euros. It's a very active market, which means it's usually easy to buy and sell without paying high fees. Some people make good money trading currencies, but it's not easy. The market can change quickly, and prices can swing up and down in a short time. That's why it's important to be cautious, learn how the market works, and build the skills needed before putting your money at risk.

A Poor Credit Score

Some people view their high credit score as a status symbol and something to be proud of. Others with a low credit score may see it as a burden that they are embarrassed to discuss. Credit scores change constantly, and there are several strategies you can employ to improve your credit score by several hundred points. I will discuss the various strategies in more detail in Commandment V (Credit and Debt). Having a perfect credit score of 850 might be a goal for some, but a credit score of 750 is still "Very Good." A good credit rating is important because it makes borrowing cheaper, impacts your ability to get an apartment, home, or car, and may even affect employment opportunities. Once you've been educated on the many strategies and tactics used to improve your credit score, you'll be surprised at how fast your score increases. The score is reflective of your financial habits and will ultimately improve the minute you improve those habits and make better financial decisions.

Retirement

Gone are the days of a nice pension at the end of our working lives, particularly for those of us who aren't from the Baby Boomer era. Honestly, I'm not sure if millennials will even have Social Security. People are living longer, yet this doesn't necessarily translate into a good quality of life. Some people may live until age 85, but may be unable to work during those last remaining years while they still have to pay bills. If you haven't planned appropriately, the money can run out before you do.

Like most things in life, if you want something done right, you have to do it yourself. This includes saving for retirement. Many of us have saved our way to millions. Start saving for retirement as early as you can. Invest in your 401(k) and take advantage of your employer's match contribution if they provide the option.

As mentioned earlier, one of the best ways to secure your financial future in retirement is to find forms of passive income. Some forms of passive income include writing a book, starting a blog, or freelancing hobby, or considering real estate investments to create more serious passive income.

Paying for College

If you have a child or are thinking of having one, you may want them to go to college. You will need to figure out how to either pay for it or help them as best you can. For most of us, paying for college outright isn't realistic, as the cost has risen 538% since 1985 per U.S. News. Today, student loan debt in the United States totals about $1.2 trillion. You would also probably like your children to move out of the house, get married, and have children of their own someday. All of those things are tough to do with overwhelming student loan debt.

There are many ways you can start saving for your child's college tuition by utilizing a 529B Savings Plan, Gerber Life Grow-Up Plan, or a host of other savings options. These plans operate like retirement accounts for college. Contribute with after-tax money or pre-tax money that's taxed when withdrawn, as long as the funds are used for educational expenses. It is important that you do not use funds set aside for retirement in your 401(k) or some other retirement vehicle for college. That would defeat the purpose and deplete your retirement savings. Most of these 529B products can also be used for your child's private school education.

FLIP THE BAG

When you can implement the principles learned from financial wisdom and instruction, you will get an influx of different ideas on how to make more money. Money is made in an infinite number of ways. Practice using the different strategies on what you already know.

Start thinking about what skills and opportunities you already have and what is needed for you to monetize them. Learn to flip the bag! As both a literal and figurative example, a few friends of mine would go to estate sales and consignment shops to find vintage luxury handbags. I didn't understand why and thought it was a waste of time. I learned that my friends would enjoy the bags for a few days and then sell them on sites that certify their authenticity. They were able to enjoy the handbags before making money off them. I had no idea that these vintage, well-preserved luxury handbags were in such high demand due to their distinctive character and high-quality craftsmanship. They used the profit from selling the bags to finance future start-up opportunities or investments. Notice, I didn't say they wasted the money on other expensive luxury items, partying, or vacations. When the goal is to flip the bag, you will find creative ways to earn additional money with the PURPOSE of investing in an idea or asset that will continue to earn you more money.

Many of us know about the secondary markets for sneakers. I remember buying the first Defining Moments Package (DMP), which were two pairs of sneakers bundled in one package for $250. I was presented with the opportunity to reserve an additional DMP at a separate store. My total costs were $500 at $250 each. I then decided to sell one DMP on the secondary market for $1,500 for a net of $1000.00 ($1,500 income - $500 costs = $1,000 net) and was able to keep a DMP for myself.

Experience is a great teacher, so I encourage you to go out into the world and utilize every possible opportunity to find discounted and undervalued items. In addition, you may already possess a skillset that allows you to add value. Experience is not gained by reading a textbook or taking a college course–in fact, by the time the information makes it into the textbook you're already too late. Get the training you need, but make sure you are finding opportunities to employ what you've learned to gain experience.

SI VIS PACEM, PARA BELLUM (IF YOU WANT PEACE, PREPARE FOR WAR)

Wisdom without action is just unrealized potential. The purpose of acquiring financial instruction is to create streams of income, prepare for future challenges, and build a secure foundation. In my own journey, I found that even small opportunities can teach valuable lessons on how to transform resources into profit while protecting myself against financial risks.

After examining several passive income strategies, I decided to invest in 1-4 unit real estate properties. I'd read books on real estate investing, spoken with real estate professionals, engaged lenders, and used underwriting spreadsheets to evaluate property metrics to avoid overpaying.

At the time, new multi-unit properties were going up all over the city, financing was accessible, and redevelopment projects– including a new school–signaled long term growth. I determined that it would be a good idea to buy an investment property in this potential development area with the expectation that the market would progress.

New construction requires a great deal of preparation, including securing financing, properly vetting the builder, building design, materials, prioritizing costs, potential upgrades, inspections, completion timeline, and proper representation throughout the buying process. Keep in mind, if you go into new construction, you must thoroughly vet the developer. Ask for a list of completed projects and client references. Check whether they finish on time and within budget. Confirm their capacity, make sure they're bonded, and seek feedback from inspectors or the municipality. A builder who asks you to finance their unfinished project is a red flag—they may not have the capital or stability to deliver.

I began working with a developer who had completed and approved plans that came close to what I was looking for. After visiting the property and seeing that the framing was up and appeared to be in good shape, I told the builder I was interested in moving forward. He asked that I finance the remainder of the project, which was an immediate red flag. It showed that he did not have the capital to complete the project and was having trouble getting additional financing. Beware of builders with partially completed properties that need buyer financing.

I walked away because I did not trust his ability to deliver. A few weeks later, I moved forward with an experienced developer who had already built new multi-family properties that I could review.

Renter demographics were another key consideration: income levels, education, employment rates, and access to transportation, to name a few.

Crime rates are also a significant consideration for safety, resale value, and insurance costs.

After closing on the property, I moved into the first unit as planned. Unfortunately, I was noticed for the wrong reasons and on multiple occasions encountered situations described in Proverbs 1:11-14.

I wore a suit and tie every day to work and drove a 550 Mercedes SUV, which drew attention in the neighborhood. One evening, I came home, opened the garage, and turned around to find someone in my car trying to drive off. Thankfully, I had the key in my pocket, so the car wouldn't move. I confronted him, and he jumped out and ran to a waiting car.

I recognized his face and later spotted him with others outside a nearby house known for shady activity. It was clear who they were and what they were doing. Even the local police seemed compromised. Rather than rely on them, I made sure they knew I wasn't afraid and would be watching.

Not long after, someone tried stealing the copper from my HVAC system. That was my breaking point. I invested in security—steel cages, bars, alarms, and reinforced doors—to protect the property and my investment.

Through this experience, I was able to apply the principles I'd learned while also gaining another important lesson: don't build a castle before building a moat. I will go deeper into this concept in Commandment VII, Protection. Before you invest, you need to carefully think through the potential risks and what you need to do to protect yourself from them. Despite the challenges, I was able to fully lease the property with qualified tenants who took great care of it. As the real estate market improved, through applying the principles and lessons learned, I was able to sell the property for a profit.

Change Your Mind, Change Your Money

"The light of the body is the eye: therefore when thine eye is single, thy whole body also is full of light; but when thine eye is evil, thy body also is full of darkness. Take heed therefore that the light which is in thee be not darkness. If thy whole body therefore be full of light, having no part dark, the whole shall be full of light, as when the bright shining of a candle doth give thee light." – Luke 11:34-36

This scripture reminds us that the way we see and interpret the world reflects what's inside of us– either light (wisdom and truth) or darkness (ignorance and confusion). Our words and actions don't just come from what we observe on the outside; they come from our inner understanding, shaped by our experiences, education, and relationship with God. When your vision—your mindset and focus—is aligned with God and guided by His Spirit, your whole life is filled with light. But if your inner wisdom is rooted in pride, fear, or anything not of God, then your thoughts and choices become distorted. A heart full of godly wisdom will naturally speak life, encouragement, truth, and love.

Remove the negative perspectives and people who lessen your light. Remove the negative feelings about yourself, others, and your current financial situation. Speak life into your finances.

Say, "I will get out of debt;" "I will own my home free and clear;" "I will be wealthy;" "I will own businesses;" "I will have multiple sources of income;" "I will be successful." Continue to brighten your light through ongoing education by seeking the wisdom of God.

"Who is a wise man and endued with
knowledge among you? let him show out
of a good conversation his works with
meekness of wisdom.
But if ye have bitter envying and strife in your
hearts, glory not, and lie not against the truth.
This wisdom descendeth not from above,
but is earthly, sensual, devilish.
For where envying and strife is, there is
confusion and every evil work.
But the wisdom that is from above is first pure,
then peaceable, gentle, and easy to be entreated,
full of mercy and good fruits, without partiality,
and without hypocrisy.
And the fruit of righteousness is sown in peace
of them that make peace." – James 3:13-18

James explains that there is a distinct difference between the wisdom of God, which is pure, peaceful, gentle, urgent, full of mercy, good fruit, impartial, and without hypocrisy, compared to earthly knowledge or values. The knowledge and ways of the world are not the wisdom of God. Therefore, be very careful to decipher earthly financial information from God's financial wisdom.

A strategic financial education must be continuous and integrated into your daily life, making the content relatable, timely, and effective as you begin to implement this information into your action plan. Once you begin to see your current financial situation as an opportunity, you will project success, prosperity, and achievement as you acquire financial wisdom. The seed of change in your money habits and a culture of financial success will start to improve any credit and debt issues as you begin to take action. The transformation of your mind is the first and most important necessary step in acquiring financial freedom. Take every opportunity to speak success into your financial situation and make sure your actions are in line with this narrative. The right financial discipline and consistent activity will yield desired financial results.

While acquiring financial information specific to your personal financial goals, continue to read financial news daily, even if you don't understand it at first. This information may be useful down the line. The more familiar you become with financial principles, the better you will be able to dissect the information at a much faster pace. Finance will get much easier to understand and can be implemented into a weekly or even daily financial routine.

Camouflage

Many of our failures come from attempting to achieve a goal or complete a task without first knowing or having all the necessary information. How can you make sound financial decisions with a limited financial education, no instruction, or financial wisdom? Go after wisdom as if it were diamonds. Not simply for the sake of having information, but to apply it liberally and wisely in every financial activity.

"This book of the law shall not depart out of thy mouth; but thou shall meditate therein day and night, that thou mayest observe to do according to all that is written therein: for then thou shalt make thy way prosperous, and then thou shalt have good success." – Joshua 1:8

The scripture employs the believer to think deeply and focus on the WORD, which is God's instruction. Meditate therein day and night. It does not say follow third-party instructions via another person's interpretation or revelation. Yes, people are a valuable resource, but you must foster a personal relationship with God and his financial instructions. The Word (Instruction) tells you to observe and DO ***all*** that is written therein. It does not say to do some of it. Only after knowing the instructions for yourself, developing a personal relationship with God, and doing ALL that is written in the Word can you then become prosperous and have success in all that you do.

Commandment II
Work

"Go to the ant, thou sluggard; consider her ways, and be wise: Which having no guide, overseer, or ruler, Provideth her meat in the summer, and gathereth her food in the harvest. How long wilt thou sleep, O sluggard? when wilt thou arise out of thy sleep? Yet a little sleep, a little slumber, a little folding of the hands to sleep: So shall thy poverty come as one that travelleth, and thy want as an armed man."
– Proverbs 6:6-12

THE ONLY WAY TO EARN A LIVING, generate wealth, and leave an inheritance to your children's children is to work.

Work doesn't just mean finding a job. Mastering your craft, creating a successful business, effectively operating your business, finding resources and funding, improving public speaking and presentation skills to earn investors' trust, and managing your brand requires a significant amount of work. Managing your time even requires work.

The key is making sure that you work on those activities that will help you accomplish your financial goals. Productivity earns income, which is key to gaining financial freedom. This may mean working more hours, taking a part-time job, or exploring entrepreneurial opportunities. Technology has made it easier than ever to start businesses and promote your products or services at a low cost. With the right tools, you can run your business more efficiently, earn higher profits, and save money as your business grows. You want to create multiple streams of passive income where your money is working for you. No one gets to this point by chance. It will take a considerable amount of work and effort. In order to have money work for you, you need to have money to put to work. Work for your money, then have your money work for you.

"For even when we were with you, this we commanded you, that if any would not work, neither should he eat. For we hear that there are some which walk among you disorderly, working not at all, but are busybodies." – 2 Thessalonians 3:10-11

It is the individual's responsibility to work and generate income. There are many forms of government assistance, from farmers' subsidies, immigrant assistance, unemployment, welfare, food stamps, tax credits, business grants, and Medicare or Medicaid. The who, what, when, where, how, and why of the government assistance debate can be tabled and revisited. The verse is important as it points to an individual's responsibility for advancing their career, business, and financial freedom. I remember my college economics professor restating a phrase from our textbook, "There is no free lunch." Everything has a cost, and the opportunity to become financially free and successful is achieved only through work.

"He becometh poor that dealeth with a slack hand: but the hand of the diligent maketh rich." – Proverbs 10:4

King Solomon is considered one of the wisest and wealthiest men to have ever lived. Gold mines were one source of King Solomon's wealth. Gold mining is a long and complex process that requires the removal, separation, and extraction of gold from non-valuable waste material. The entire process takes diligence. Therefore, on our journey through the wealth creation cycle, it is imperative that you identify and remove all of the waste and immaterial excess information, habits, behaviors, thoughts, and people from your daily life in order to be successful. Your work and service need to be thorough and complete. A lazy work product and a poor reputation signify a poor work ethic and will lead to poverty. The Word instructs us to do excellent work.

TALENTS

Matthew 25:14-30 reads, *"For the kingdom of heaven is as a man travelling into a far country, who called his own servants, and delivered unto them his goods. And unto one he gave five talents, to another two, and to another one; to every man according to his several ability; and straightway took his journey."*

*"Then he that had received the five talents went and **traded** with the same, and made them other five talents. And likewise he that had received two, he also gained other two. But he that had received one went and digged in the earth, and hid his lord's money."*

When the lord returned to reconcile with his servants, the one he had given five talents provided the additional five. The lord said, *"Well done, thou good and faithful servant: thou hast been faithful over a few things, I will make thee ruler over many things: enter thou into the joy of thy lord."* The servant who received two talents addressed the lord saying, *"Lord, thou deliverdst unto me two talents: behold, I have gained two other talents beside them."* His lord replied to this servant in the same manner stating, *"Well done, good and faithful servant; thou hast been faithful over a few things, I will make thee ruler over many things: enter thou into the joy of thy lord."*

Notice that the response is the same for each servant despite the amount of talent each servant was blessed with. His response is the same: "Well done, good and faithful servant: thou hast been faithful over a few things, I will make thee ruler over many things: enter thou into the joy of thy lord."

It's important to understand that we are all born with unique talents, according to our many abilities, which include physical, intellectual, social, spiritual, financial, or any combination.

God provides these gifts and blessings with the expectation that you will multiply them. Once you've done so and proven yourself to be faithful with what God has already provided, He will make you ruler over many things.

Stop worrying, agonizing, stressing, hating on other people, minding everyone else's business, or thinking about what talents God has given others. Focus on the talents God has given you. When you multiply your talents, He will bless you in the same manner in which he has those who are perceived to have more.

You may have parents, relatives, or even a spouse who act as dream busters, never encouraging you and projecting their insecurities onto you. They may have fears that prevent them from accomplishing their goals, are always negative, frequently invite you to their pity party, are small-minded, low frequency, and always have ongoing issues for seemingly no apparent reason. If these people are around you, remove yourself from this toxic environment.

By the same token, if God has blessed you with significant talents, don't parade about as though you're better, privileged, or more important. Focus only on multiplying your talents, because if you are not faithful with what God has given you, He will not make you ruler over many things, regardless of the talents you possess.

Now, the last servant who received one talent made excuses for why he was unable to multiply the talent God gave him. He even blamed the lord and allowed fear and lack of effort to paralyze him.

Matthew 25:24-30, *"Then he which had received the one talent came and said, Lord, I knew thee that thou art an hard man, reaping where thou hast not sown, and gathering where thou hast not strowed: And I was afraid, and went and hid thy talent in the earth: lo, there thou hast that is thine."*

The Lord's response to this servant was considerably different from the other two. *"His lord answered and said unto him, Thou wicked and slothful servant, thou knewest that I reap where I sowed not, and gather where I have not strowed: Thou oughtest therefore to have put my money to the **exchangers**, and then at my coming I should have received mine own with* *usury (interest). Take therefore the talent from him, and give it unto him which hath ten talents. For unto every one that hath shall be given, and he shall have abundance: but from him that hath not shall be taken away even that which he hath. And cast ye the* **unprofitable** *servant into outer darkness: there shall be weeping and gnashing of teeth."*

The servant's choice to bury his gifts, intelligence, money, and God-given ability yielded no return on God's initial investment. Instead of using his talent to multiply his blessings, where he would be made ruler over many things, he buried his talent and wasted it away. The servant was labeled wicked and lazy.

The phrase *'reaping where I have not sown and gathering where I have not strowed'* reflects the role of the lord as a powerful figure, like a wealthy business owner or investor, who provides resources and expects a return on that investment. As a business owner, he expects his employees to perform and grow the business. As an investor, he is relying on the business owners or entrepreneurs to do the work and generate a sufficient return. In this example, the servant failed to manage the resources entrusted to him by the Lord, who represents someone with financial wisdom. The Lord even offered practical advice, suggesting that, at the very least, the money could have been placed in a foreign currency exchange or investment to earn interest.

The servant with one talent made another critical mistake. He did not ask the servants who multiplied their blessings for advice. Instead, he watched others gain success and stayed on the sidelines. He didn't even try! Given they all were servants of the same master, it's highly likely the successful servants would've gladly helped if asked.

If someone is succeeding in the exact area you want to grow in, don't hesitate to reach out and ask for their guidance. If they say no, move on to the next person until you get the help you need. Rejection is something you must get used to if you're going to be successful. Caring successful people are always willing to provide advice and feedback. You just need to find them.

The saying, "scared money don't make money" is very true. There are always risks associated with making money. The greater your expertise and experience, the more comfortable you are in taking those calculated risks. The servant, paralyzed by fear and having no initiative, chose a course of inaction which he considered to be safe. In fact, it was the riskiest decision, and it ended with everything being taken away.

What might feel unsettling about this passage is that the servant's actions led to his gifts being taken away and given to the one who already had the most. This is exactly what happens in the real world. Complain about it all you want. This commandment is one of the laws of money, and the consequence is that what you have will be taken from you and given to someone else who is able to multiply it. Essentially, you will be replaced by someone who can do a better job. Stop sitting on your blessings and work to multiply them before they are taken away.

> *"In all labour there is profit: but the talk of the lips tendeth only to penury (poverty)."*
> *– Proverbs 14:23*

Unsuccessful people sure have a lot to say. People who don't have jobs want to provide employment advice. Those who aren't married want to provide marriage advice. Individuals without children want to tell you how to raise your kids. Renters want to teach you how to buy a house or how to own rental property. Individuals who have never been business owners want to show you how to run your business. People with no money, or outside of the finance industry with no experience, want to tell you how to make money and where to invest it. As the saying goes, "talk is cheap." Your deeds are what matter, and they should be closely aligned with your words. It's so much easier to talk than to do the actual work. Doing the work required to be successful can be painful and requires enormous effort. A lazy, slothful person would rather talk. Be committed to doing the work.

THE VEIL OF EASY MONEY (TAKE THE LONG ROAD)

When I was twelve years old, my mom purchased a basketball hoop for me and had a blacktop installed in the backyard, which was amazing considering my love of basketball. My friends and other neighborhood kids would often come play.

One day, a kid I'd never met before came over to play while I was playing by myself. We began shooting around. He was younger, but we still had a good time. The kid wasn't dressed to play basketball. He was wearing nice clothes and sneakers. When we took a break after an hour of nonstop play, instead of asking me for a towel or some water, he began wiping off his face with a huge stack of money he pulled from his pocket.

"You should come work for me," he said.

"No thank you," I replied. He then attempted to hand me the stack of money. "I'm good," I replied again.

The young kid had no idea what he had really gotten himself into, nor could he fully grasp the depth of his behavior. He was obviously in the company of individuals who believed money was easy to get and knew where there was an abundance of it. I didn't know if he came over on his own or was sent to recruit me. Either way, that was a game I decided not to play.

Fast money has severe consequences. The long road to earning money may be much slower, but it's the best way to ensure safe, sustainable results. In order to take the long road, you have to do the work to develop your craft and enhance your skills.

Droppin Dimes

In high school, I recognized the need to improve my basketball skills, but I didn't know how. Without a clear guide or manual on what steps to take, I asked a coach if he could help me work on certain areas of my game outside of regular practice. He agreed, but never showed up. I realized then that wanting to improve is one thing, but knowing how to improve and having someone show you is something entirely different.

Looking back, I didn't understand how many hours of focused effort it takes to rise above the competition. I should have been in the gym at 6 a.m., running drills before school, then heading to convocation by 8. After a full day of classes, I had team practice, and afterward, I still should've been getting shots up and refining my skills. I know now that becoming great at something requires working at it multiple times a day. But no one told me that then. I didn't work hard enough, and there was no one there to show me what it took to become the player I aspired to be.

The same is true when it comes to financial success. How many hours are required to become successful and achieve your financial goals? At a minimum, 4 hours a day. A typical day would involve waking up at 5 a.m. to get ahead, or 4 a.m. if you want to exercise, and going to bed around 10 p.m. Create a schedule to allocate time for improvement and stick to it. Find time to listen to financial education during your daily commute, while eating lunch, at the gym, waiting in line, cooking, and during downtime. Put the time in.

Sweat Equity

The early years of my banking career felt like a simpler time, full of optimism and free from the mistakes that would later define the era depicted in *Too Big to Fail*, a book by Andrew Ross Sorkin chronicling the 2008 financial crisis. Those mistakes, including reckless subprime lending and risky banking practices, led to the second-largest financial collapse in U.S. history since the Great Depression. Because the largest banks were so interconnected, the government had to step in with a $700 billion bailout, officially known as the Troubled Asset Relief Program (TARP), to buy distressed assets and stabilize the economy. Before all of that unfolded, I was working for the largest credit card issuer in the world.

The founder graduated from my High School, St. Benedict's Prep in Newark, NJ, where the bank had opened its newest location. Despite being a very large bank, culturally, it was reminiscent of the 80s sitcom Cheers with the closeness of a small-town family-owned restaurant bar. I was in the most recent class of credit underwriters and had room for improvement. My goal was to accurately assess each applicant's creditworthiness and, when approved, assign an appropriate credit limit to their account. Customers needed me to fairly assess their ability to repay and the bank needed me to minimize exposure to default risk.

To improve, I stayed long hours after work with my manager going over hundreds of additional credit scenarios and applications to gain more experience. My manager made himself available to help me improve, providing detailed explanations for why I made the correct decision and why other decisions were incorrect. Even making the right decision for the wrong reason can lead to inconsistency, low productivity, and reflect poorly on your skillset. In this role, success is measured by your ability to consistently make sound decisions based on large amounts of information with accuracy and efficiency. Making the correct decisions for the right reasons made me a better analyst. Credit approval authority carries an important responsibility. It's as much art as it is science. Putting in the work helped advance my career.

The amount of time spent on improvement needs to match the desired results. The process of improvement through self-help, training and mentorship centers around the number of productive hours you are willing to spend getting better.

Guns and Butter

The contention between the use of nitrates, a concentrated mixture of nitric and sulfuric acids, for gun powder (guns) or fertilizers to create more food (butter) originated in 1916 with the passage of the National Defense Act as the country began preparing to enter World War I. Over time, the expression "guns and butter" has been used to more concisely debate the allocation of government spending on the military versus other important domestic priorities. The President of the United States and Congress set the fiscal budget annually, where the effects and potential consequences of future geopolitical economics are used to determine the frequency and severity of conflict.

The relationship between war efforts and the increase in GDP per capita (by head count) by decreasing unemployment through wartime production has inconsistent results. Instability will usually depress economic growth in countries impacted by conflict which are likely strategic in regards to timing. The advantages of creating unstable macroeconomic environments places the antagonist in a financial position of power in a global economy. Economic warfare, particularly when coupled with physical military efforts, attempts to weaken an adversary's economy by disrupting and denying physical, health, financial, and technological resources through inhibiting the benefits of trade in addition to undermining the country's ability to operate normally. If you can beat them, destroy their economy so they can never effectively retaliate.

The time and effort (work) spent on guns—material resources including intelligence, people, suspension of aid, embargos, and propaganda to effectively restrict the country's ability to produce goods internally or through trade with other countries—is an expensive undertaking.

Contrarily, the amount of work spent on infrastructure, education, jobs, manufacturing, technology, energy, and strong financial markets creates an environment that increases GDP per capita and a future for strong economic growth. Subsidies, tax breaks, grants, and government incentives in industries identified for growth give direction to the free market on what businesses to create and where job growth is expected in order for the country to compete globally.

Decisions on how to shape the country's economic position within the next 5-10 years are reflected in the type of focus on current efforts in areas like healthcare innovation, education reform, demographic shifts, infrastructure development, and economic policies. Or, we could just spend most of our efforts fighting and stealing resources.

The movie Baby Boy, released in 2001, was about a young man forced to address his priorities and commitments in challenging, yet unfortunately self-inflicted, circumstances. Written and directed by John Singleton, the main character is jobless with two children by two different women and living at home with his mother. The mother's love interest attempts to provide advice to the aspiring business owner and his friend explaining the difference between guns and butter. In the movie, guns represent real estate, stocks, bonds, investments, art, and assets that appreciate over time. The butter represented items that do not store value like cars, clothes, and jewelry. The main character was urged to focus his time and effort (work) on acquiring assets that appreciate and are income-producing.

In your own personal economic microecosystem, there is contention between guns and butter. Where you put the most effort will determine your level of success. Time is extremely valuable. Determine your financial destination. Figure out where you want to be financially and what you need to accomplish in the next 5-10 years. Break this down into what you need to do every month, every week, and every day to accomplish your financial goals. Outline the number of hours it will take each day to complete your tasks. Focus on making sure every behavior and relationship has purpose specifically aligning with your daily, weekly, and monthly efforts to achieve each financial goal.

We can't even get into the airport without a plane ticket that shows the destination. There are multiple checkpoints that make sure you have a boarding pass. Along the way there are signs leading you to the correct terminal with terminal staff ready to assist if there is any confusion. On the way to your gate, there will be many distractions. Stay focused, don't miss your flight wandering around the newly remodeled terminal. Everyone is there for the same reason. We've identified where we need to go. It's going to cost you time and money but it's well worth the investment.

Put your time and effort (work) into the right areas on your journey toward financial success. Be aware that the mental and physical effort needed to achieve a desired result is nothing without purpose. Let me reiterate, every behavior and action must be aligned.

KEYS TO STAYING THE COURSE

Be Introspective

You should assess weekly whether you are evolving into the person you must become in order to be successful. The new evolved version of yourself may have to be someone who doesn't get much sleep to reach your goals. Don't wait for an annual review from your employer, a negative review from a customer, shade from a family member or friend, or a bad business deal to put the battery in your back. Stay motivated! Be meticulous and perfect your craft. Create a daily schedule of goals and work to accomplish them. Identify three or four critical objectives to complete each day. Ensure the tasks are manageable, add value, and contribute to your long-term goals.

Get Organized

Stop multitasking or switching. Switching from task to task within seconds or minutes lowers intellect, inhibits emotional intelligence, slows you down, increases stress, and increases mistakes. Be diligent in completing each task and reap the fruit of seeds sown. Focus is a fundamental quality of successful and productive people. Our brains are wired to work best when we focus on a single task. Practice staying focused and strive to complete one task before diving into another. The challenges of the day may often make it difficult to stay focused, and juggling multiple responsibilities is a part of life. The better organized you are, the easier it will be to handle these various responsibilities and prevent you from feeling overwhelmed.

Manage Interruptions

Manage interruptions to stay on track and accomplish your goals. People often minimize or forget how many times they were interrupted throughout the day. Interruptions can come in all forms including clients, co-workers, peers, and family.

To better manage interruptions, keep a stack of Post-it notes or index cards nearby with the names of people who commonly disrupt your workflow. First, identify those who are likely to interrupt with legitimate needs—team members, clients, or colleagues who may need quick input or guidance. Anticipate their questions and jot down possible responses ahead of time. This helps you address their concerns quickly and efficiently, reducing the frequency and duration of their interruptions.

Next, make note of those whose interruptions tend to derail your focus entirely—those who pull you off task with unrelated conversations or non-urgent issues. For these individuals, avoid engagement at that moment. Instead, check off their names as a reminder to respond once your critical tasks for the day are complete.

There will always be distractions, and while some are welcome, others act as tranquilizers, leaving you stagnant and barbiturate with a "Dream Deferred."

Finish What You Start

Make sure you finish! Creating a list of objectives is worthless if you lack the discipline to complete every task. Many of us are great starters but fall short of finishing. How many times have you started a project or task, and had to take it off your to-do list instead of pushing through and completing every item? Keep a journal of completed projects and tasks to catalogue instances where you've accomplished your goals. Review what contributed to this success and replicate.

Set Milestones

Set milestones for large projects so you're not overwhelmed. Break large projects into mini-tasks and set individual success metrics to improve your morale and keep energy levels high.

Record your progress, reward yourself, and share your progress with those important people involved. Share your wins with people who are very encouraging. Always be sure to celebrate interim achievements.

FORGETFUL HEARER

"For if any be a hearer of the word, and not a doer, he is like unto a man beholding his natural face in a glass: For he beholdeth himself, and goeth his way, and straightway forgetteth what manner of man he was. But whoso looketh into the perfect law of liberty, and continueth therin, he being not a forgetful hearer, but a doer of the work, this man shall be blessed in his deed." – James 1:23-25

Financial captivity is passed down through generations. This is why the hearer who sees himself in the mirror goes his way, forgetting the diligence, hard work, process, and habits that will make him successful. Even delayed obedience, or subtle disobedience, has severe consequences. Generations who have been deceived pass down a culture that reinforces a mindset of financial captivity. The only thing the enemy needs to do to pull you away from God is to systematically program one generation in order to pass down the curse of poverty, lack, and debt. The hearer of the word, who is not forgetful, but a doer of the work, will be blessed.

The Bible gives us a blueprint for how to succeed in all areas of personal finance. Biblical financial principles require an obedient doer in order to access God's abundance. The right and true pathway to financial freedom requires the suppression of lust for material items, satisfying the flesh through sinful behavior, and managing distractions that pull you away from focusing on the work needed to accomplish your goals.

"For though we walk in the flesh, we do not war after the flesh: (For the weapons of our warfare are not carnal, but mighty through God to the pulling down of strong holds;) Casting down imaginations, and every high thing that exalteth itself against the knowledge of God, and bringing into captivity every thought to the obedience of Christ; And having in a readiness to revenge all disobedience, when your obedience is fulfilled." – 2 Corinthians 10:3-7

Obedience to the will of God is your revenge. This is the only way to overcome life's many challenges. Obedience shows an ability to handle the financial breakthrough that will activate both God's covering and financial blessings. This vital part of the process cannot be overlooked. At times, you may put in the work, yet the blessing is still blocked because of disobedience. In full submission, God will lead you down the right path and redirect your efforts. God will not put you in an important high position if He believes you will turn away from Him.

Commandment III
Budget

"For which of you, intending to build a tower, sitteth not down first, and counteth the cost, whether he have sufficient to finish it? Lest haply, after he hath laid the foundation, and is not able to finish it, all that behold it begin to mock him, saying, This man began to build, and was not able to finish." – *Luke 14:28-30*

A WELL-MANAGED BUDGEt is your roadmap to financial success. The most successful businesses, organizations, and people rely on an accurate financial plan in order to achieve their goals.

A budget gives you a clear roadmap before you take action, helping you plan effectively, make adjustments, and communicate your goals with anyone supporting your financial journey. A budget provides a needed framework at inception before any real work begins.

Many of us hate the idea of living on a budget because of the misconception that budgets deprive us of everything we enjoy. To the contrary, a budget actually allows us to live our best lives. Having a financial plan requires discipline, but it's designed to help you accomplish your goals and live your dreams without yielding to the millions of daily distractions.

If you look back at those goals you have yet to accomplish, there is always a perfectly timed distraction that has inhibited you from moving forward. Every distraction moves you farther from your financial goals, increasing the risk of missing out on God's abundance and ability to live life to the fullest. Success is the result of proper planning and positive activity. The benefits of a budget far outweigh the work involved in creating one.

Everything in life begins with purpose. Whether you are looking to purchase new clothes, furniture, an automobile, a home, pay for school, eliminate debt, start a new business, or set any other new financial goal, working toward your purpose through having a budget is essential to enjoying God's blessings. Show God you can handle what He's already entrusted to you, so He can bless you abundantly.

Individuals with strong money management skills have a financial plan and the discipline to achieve financial success. The most successful companies have a budget. A business is no more than an extension of the individuals who own it. The company's financial health is a reflection of management's abilities, or inabilities, to make sound financial decisions. This is why banks consistently assess a company's management when determining the company's viability. The company's financial statements are reflective of the decisions made to achieve financial success.

Look at yourself as though you were a brand or business. The more successful you are at managing your personal finances, the more successful you'll be at running your family finances like a business. Companies with a strong financial foundation have plenty of cash, low debt, and valuable assets, making them stable and well-prepared for tough times. Running your personal finances in the same way will help you reach the end goal of being asset wealthy and cash rich. Many of us have never learned how to successfully create and live by a budget. In this section, I will show you a simple way to create a budget and share strategies on how to stick to it.

HOW TO CREATE YOUR BUDGET

The following section walks you through how to create a simple budget. Visit https://10coincommandments.com to get a free digital workbook to guide you with your budget creation.

Income

At the top of your budget, list all sources of income for the month, including your salary from your primary job, any other employment, and all other sources of income. Depending on the various types and sources of income, which may come with incentives, your monthly income may fluctuate. If so, take the average of the last three months. It's important to remove inconsistent non-recurring income as it's better to underestimate income rather than to overestimate income. Take-home pay (money earned after taxes, retirement, and insurance deductions), not gross income, is where you need to start.

Fixed Expenses

Fixed Expenses, like a mortgage, rent, car payment, and car insurance, do not fluctuate each month. For businesses, a fixed expense does not vary based on production or sales levels. It's important to minimize the number of fixed expenses you have because it's harder to eliminate this type of expense to increase savings or mitigate a loss of income. Remember to include infrequent, non-monthly fixed expenses like car registration or rental insurance in the annual budget. If you would rather reflect this as a monthly expense to better allocate resources for when these expenses are due, divide the expense (car registration) by twelve and save this amount each month until it's due.

Variable Expenses

Variable Expenses occur regularly and can also be necessary expenses, but you have much more control over how much you spend. These expenses include groceries, phone bill, electricity, heating, gas, transportation expenses, internet, childcare expenses, and household supplies. Variable expenses can be adjusted if there is a sudden change to your financial situation. Variable expenses can be decreased to manageable amounts without severely sacrificing your standard of living to accomplish specific saving goals or to accommodate adjusting to a lower income.

Discretionary Expenses

A discretionary expense is simply money you choose to spend but don't necessarily need to spend. Discretionary expenses include clothing, entertainment, dining out, recreation, vacation, hair care, snacks, coffee, luxury goods, and other nonessential items. After successfully tracking your spending for 30 days, you will find that these discretionary expenses are the first items you will adjust to increase savings.

Since fixed expense items are more difficult to change, look for ways to decrease your variable and discretionary expenses in addition to finding multiple ways to increase your income. As you formulate a financial plan, you will begin to realize that you can no longer afford everything you want to buy and have to make tradeoffs. Making tradeoffs may mean giving up consumption of some of your favorite items or buying less expensive sale items to increase your net income.

Create a budget you can live with that is realistic and allows some flexibility for adjusting to changes in income or expenses. After creating your budget, remember you will have to adjust your projections every month, so be patient. After a few months of adjustments, you should be able to accurately project how much you are likely to spend in a given month.

Payment Priorities

When allocating after-tax income, the first priority is to pay your monthly household bills. There are many potential penalties for late payments, such as late fees, loss of items purchased with credit, eviction, or falling behind on your mortgage.

Next, set aside money you'll need for your daily expenses each week. Planning for these expenses, like groceries, public transportation, and gas can help you stay on track with your spending budget. If you've projected how much money you should be spending on these variable and discretionary expenses, the budget will help keep you on track if you begin to overspend. This is going to require the use of some form of tracking system, likely provided by your bank via debit card transactions. Several banks have budget monitoring alerts that email or text you when you're close to or have gone over your budget.

Emergency Fund

Once income is allocated to cover your regular expenses, start working on building an emergency fund by saving three to six months of take-home pay for unexpected emergencies. The emergency fund protects against issues that may result in a setback to your financial goals. Having three to six months in reserves helps you manage a loss of income due to issues like layoffs, loss of clients, or a slow period in your business. It's important to have enough income to cover fixed, variable, and discretionary expenses for three to six months because that might be just enough income to sustain yourself or the business while working through any difficulties to get back on your feet. Obviously, the more months you have saved to cover expenses, the more time you have if there is an issue in producing income. After saving three to six months of take-home pay, begin saving for other emergencies like the need to replace a water heater or HVAC repair, a new roof, car repair, sudden medical expenses, and various childcare expenses.

Save so that random life events don't derail you while working to accomplish your financial goals. It's impossible to invest in yourself, a great idea, or a partnership if you haven't saved for these emergencies. After such emergencies are reasonably accounted for, think about how much is required to invest in your future. This could be investing in multiple retirement vehicles, saving start-up capital for your small business, or allocating money required to invest in a partnership for future business opportunities. We'll talk in more detail about emergency funds in the next commandment.

STRATEGIES FOR STICKING TO YOUR BUDGET

Auto Pilot

Once you've gotten a solid handle on your budget, continue to review and make any necessary adjustments. Don't be complacent by operating on autopilot. Automating your finances is a good idea, particularly if you've struggled paying your bills on time, are forgetful, or don't open your mail frequently. However, you must constantly re-evaluate your financial situation because the economy is cyclical and always changing. Your financial goals should continue to evolve with every progression, achievement, and in-depth review of your financial picture.

Spending Traps

When purchasing a particular item, consider whether you really need it or if it's just something you want. Think about what need you are looking to fulfill through the purchase. Can you spend money on the item and still cover your monthly expenses? The reality and root of compulsive spending must be addressed as your finances are just a reflection of the decisions you make. Some root causes of compulsive spending habits may be traced back to your childhood. You might waste money on luxury handbags because you grew up in a household where your parents couldn't afford to buy you luxury items. Now, you see these items as status symbols or representations of success. As a result, your worth and value are based on those luxury items, where you believe that others may be more receptive of you once you've obtained them.

I'm not against certain lifestyle choices if you're living within your means. However, spending on items you don't really need–or sometimes don't even want–to make yourself feel better is dangerous. Think about this: Is it possible you're looking for acceptance through clothes or handbags because of early childhood or teen rejection for not having the most up-to-date clothes and accessories?

Men, are you still buying sneakers as an adult because you didn't have them growing up? Instead of dressing for your future as an entrepreneur, CEO, CFO, COO, or real estate investment property owner, your attire may be reflective of who you wished you were growing up. Owning a few pairs of your favorite sneakers is fine. However, possessing an excessive amount means something deeper may need to be addressed.

I once collected sneakers and have several pairs in my closet that have never been worn. I remember asking God for a promotion, and He revealed that I was more focused on wasting time and money on who I used to be than preparing for my future blessings. As a result, I worked to improve my skillset and purchased clothes that let God know I was ready for my promotion. I could not expect the respect of men while I was dressed as a child. You are what you wear. I needed to transform my mind so that my behaviors and how I presented myself aligned with my goals.

People dress in a manner that reveals their perception of themselves. Wasteful spending and poor financial decisions that hurt your future require a re-evaluation of your priorities. Determine if you're living for yourself and your family, or looking for acceptance from people who don't care about you at all.

Is your spending behavior masking an insecurity or a way of coping with depression? Did you spend compulsively because you were having a bad day and thought it would make you feel better at that moment? Clothing and luxury items are not the only means by which money can be wasted. People also purchase other items, like food, to relieve stress. Emotions and moods can affect our spending behavior, whether it be the guilt of not spending money to support an elementary school candy sale, envy from trying to keep up with the Joneses, sadness, fear propaganda that suggests someone is going to take away your gun rights, or stock market advice that an undervalued stock should be purchased before it explodes in value. A budget helps to overcome compulsive spending and keeps you moving towards your financial goals.

Purchasing Considerations

Research to determine when, how, and where to buy products to get the best deal. Research product claims to separate fact from fantasy advertising. Check product ratings and reviews in magazines and online. Visit the store and ask for a product demonstration to get familiar with the product before you buy. Give a thorough inspection of the product you have an interest in purchasing. Ask for advice from friends and family familiar with the product you're considering. If you doubt the product's quality and durability, stick to brand names. It's also important to check warranties so you understand what's covered and for how long, where applicable.

Use the internet to comparison shop to save time and transportation costs before going to see products. The goal is not to simply find an item at the lowest price because you often get what you pay for. The objective is purchase value, which includes good customer service, company reputation, return policy, and a fair price. Watch for sales, coupons, and rebate offers to get the best possible price.

There is a difference between deciding you want to purchase an item and searching for the lowest price versus compulsive spending when you notice a sale. In the latter circumstance, the retail company is trying to trick you into spending money you didn't plan on spending by strategically wording the purchase as saving money (40% off, save $100). In reality, you spend less on the item, but you do not save anything. Remember, saving only occurs when your savings and investment accounts increase.

Income Forecasting

The Consumer Price Index (CPI) measures how prices of goods and services change over time. The CPI is a way to measure inflation. The prices of eggs, milk, and your home gas and electric bill have likely increased tremendously over the past few years. Everyone is feeling the increase in groceries and other necessary expenses. If you're not effectively working on a plan to make more money (forecasting), then you're in big trouble. At some point, finding different ways to lower expenses won't be enough.

On average, the inflation rate in the US is approximately 3% annually. This is far less than the 7% inflation rate reported between 2021-2022. In any case, you need to figure out ways to make more money, or your dollars will not outpace inflation. Can you increase your income by 10% annually? The issue is likely not that you can't increase your annual income by 10% but that you never thought to do so.

The first step is to create a new projected budget for next year. In the income section, increase your current income by 10%. If you have a 401(k), think about increasing your contribution, especially if the company will match. Spend time putting together a plan to acquire the required education, skills, and licenses needed to increase your income. These new skills may require some initial investment, but they will be an income multiplier. It's likely you already have the skills needed to increase your income, but you need to channel these abilities in the right direction. Create daily, weekly, and monthly goals to get you to this 10% increase. This may include a promotion, raise, bonus, changing your employer, or the start of a new side business. Think through the combination of factors that will get you to your goal. On average, changing jobs every two to three years can increase your annual salary by 10% - 20% compared to staying in the same position. Figure out a plan that will allow you to increase your income by 10% by year's end.

The fiscally responsible way to save more money is by continuing to spend at the same level, allowing you to actually save the increase. Purpose, focus, and support will set you up for God's overflow. After you've increased your income by 10%, allocate the increase in your bonus, salary, part-time job income, side hustle income, business income, tax return income, or all of the above to savings. The goal is not to make more money to spend. The goal is to allocate money towards investment opportunities that will multiply your money.

The next goal is to increase your income by 20%. It's not as difficult as it sounds, but it will take a sharper focus and a significant shift in mindset from being a consumer to a more efficient producer of a good or service. Success is only as strong as the plan behind it. Write down 100 ways you can make money to increase your income by 20%. Start with a top ten. Write down the next ten. Keep going until you reach 100. To help you brainstorm, think through the different aspects of a business life cycle from material supply, production, communication, marketing, advertising, lending, banking, payroll, treasury management services, real estate, equipment, transportation, shipping, distribution, sales, legal services, customer service, employee training, and technology to name a few. There are more than 100 ways in which money is made in each business. Identify where you fit into the equation. Are your skills transferable to multiple industries?

Self-Investment

"But this I say, He which soweth sparingly shall reap also sparingly; and he which soweth bountifully shall reap also bountifully." – 2 Corinthians 9:6

The context of the scripture encourages us to be cheerful givers to others according to what's in our hearts without reluctance or necessity. The blessings of God to the giver include grace and sufficiency in all things.

However, I want you to look at the verse in isolation without context. The most important giver in your life is you. The only person responsible for your future is you. Put maximum effort into your character, personal development, education, skills, career, business, and financial health. A budget is the plan for your personal financial investment. If every dollar earned goes out the door within hours of receipt, you are investing in something or someone outside of yourself. Invest bountifully in yourself so that you can also reap bountifully. The sooner you begin to invest in yourself, the more this investment will grow. Make abundant financial investments into your future and stay consistent over time. This requires ongoing financial education to keep up with the many changes in investment strategies. Wise counsel is important, but you are solely responsible for your future financial health.

TEACH YOUR CHILDREN

"Train up a child in the way he should go: and when he is old, he will not depart from it." – Proverbs 22:6

As parents, we have the opportunity to educate our children about the importance of money management. Teaching our children to develop a healthy relationship with money will break generational curses, have a positive life-long impact, and provide the necessary financial wisdom needed to make them successful adults. While teaching your children sound money management, you will also improve your knowledge, skills, and attitudes toward money.

As soon as your child can count, introduce them to money. When you take your children shopping, introduce them to the concept of spending versus saving. As we all know, children have no problem reminding you of what you said was the right thing to do. This will keep you committed to the financial culture you are establishing at home. Explain to them how money is used to store, measure, and exchange value.

As you teach your children about money, gradually transfer financial responsibility to them so that they gain experience in planning, making the right choices, and learn to be financially independent. It's important that your kids hear your perspective on money. Make money a daily conversation. Engage your child in age-appropriate conversations about money. Share some of your money-saving strategies. Discuss aspects of family financial planning, such as how you were able to accomplish paying for a family vacation. Also, explain some of the mistakes you've made with money and how you've learned from them. It's best to help your children learn from your mistakes so they don't have to experience the same setback. When you don't educate your children on previous mistakes, generational curses persist through ignorance.

Set financial goals with your children by encouraging them to put money they've made through an allowance or a part-time job in an interest-earning account like a Certificate of Deposit (CD) or Money Market account. An allowance, no matter the size, allows them to make their own decisions, forcing them to live with any poor choices. Having to deal with the consequences of their own decisions at a young age provides an opportunity for correction and experience with the emotional burden of poor financial choices. Use the allowance to help them understand the difference between needs and wants. Spending priorities through a budget will guide them through the week. The child should be required to save a portion of the allowance each week.

Build your child's credit profile by either opening a joint credit card or adding them to your existing credit card account. My mother added me to her American Express Credit Card account in 1998. If the credit card is opened in the teen's name, get a low-limit card while they are in high school. Credit cards can build their credit profile, provide financial flexibility and convenience. However, it must be closely managed because kids can definitely get into trouble. Teach them how to manage a credit card account, particularly by saving their receipts, viewing and checking their monthly statements, and having them charge only what they can pay off completely each month with no revolving balance. In learning how to manage debt early, they will likely be able to manage debt as adults.

Encourage your children to give to charitable causes. Ask them to consider what causes they care about and how they would like to make a difference in the world. Talk to your children about the different types of donation requests and ask for their input on where the family should contribute. Encourage your children to volunteer with you on various community service projects. Volunteering is a powerful experience for both parents and children, recognizing community needs and the benefits of giving back.

A child knowing how to create a budget and save money is the critical first step to financial independence and wealth creation. An introduction to financial institutions' products and services initiates relationships in the banking world that will serve them on the road to financial success, with you being their example.

"He that is faithful in that which is least is faithful also in much: and he that is unjust in the least is unjust also in much."
– Luke 16:10

Commandment IV
Save

"Give a portion to seven, and also to eight;
for thou knowest not what evil shall be
upon the earth." – Ecclesiastes 11:2

THE BIBLE VERSE INSTRUCTS YOU to save as much as seven to eight times your income, crops, and livestock. The best translation for today's economy would be for a person to have eight months of total expenses saved. "Evil" in the verse pertains to famine, disease, adverse weather conditions, hyperinflation, and war. God wants you to be prepared for the many trials that may impact your finances in the future. This call to save is God providing a covering for his people.

Don't spend all of your blessings at once. Some of these blessings will be needed to sustain you in the future. Saving is an act of faith we often miss. God wants to protect us in difficult times. Emergencies like job loss, increased prices due to changes in the economy, unexpected medical expenses, and caring for elderly parents all have an effect on our finances. Saving is an act of faith, stewardship, and preparation. Adhere to God's instructions and save!

HOW TO BUILD YOUR SAVINGS

Saving Means Not Spending

Saving money can feel overwhelming, especially when you're unsure where those extra dollars will come from. Yet, there's always a way to save more money, and it starts with adjustments to your behavior and giving your money purpose. Once purpose is assigned to your money, adjusting your behavior will follow suit as certain habits will no longer align with your current financial strategy.

Get control of your financial plan by tracking how, when, and where you spend your money. Being fully aware of your cash outflows is an important step to gathering vital information needed to create your financial road map or budget. Spend the next 30 days, with pen and pad or on your phone, writing down when and where you spend money and how much money you spend. Meticulously record each item down to the penny. If you don't want to carry a pen and pad everywhere, use your debit card and track every swipe, reviewing your charges daily.

What you hope to find through tracking are opportunities to save. You may come to realize that a daily ritual—like buying coffee—is costing you far more than you thought. Reducing the frequency or cutting a habit outright can add thousands of dollars to your savings. Determine whether you're buying products or services you actually need or even use, or whether there is a way to find the product or service for less.

I was spending approximately $7.00 every morning on breakfast. Granted, I worked in NYC, and prices are abnormally high for a turkey, bacon, egg, and cheese on a buttered roll ($4.75) with a bottle of water ($2.00) plus tax at that time. Even when I would get a large oatmeal ($4.00) and a bottle of water, there wasn't much of a difference. I came out a little better when ordering a bagel with butter and jelly ($1.75) and bottled water ($2.00).

Once I started tracking this expense, I realized that I was spending $176.00 a month and $2,112.00 a year on breakfast. In addition, my lunch expenses averaged $15.00 a day, $330.00 a month, and $3,960.00 a year. If I continued to purchase breakfast and lunch each day, I would spend $6,072.00 a year on food during my workdays.

I realized I needed to figure out a way to cut into that number and save the money I was spending on eating out. I wasn't wasting money on a habit like buying coffee multiple times a day, but I did find that I could adjust my breakfast and lunch spending habits to increase my savings.

After seeing how much I was spending on eating out for breakfast and lunch, my adjustment became obvious. Preparing food at home would save me a lot of money. I'm fortunate that my wife is an excellent cook, and she began packing my lunch every day. My lunch was usually leftovers from the previous night, but it would sometimes be a different meal altogether. My wife would tell me, "If you're going to the moon, let me pack you a moon lunch." To be efficient, we made adjustments in our grocery purchases and used coupons and sales to save money on food. Committing to a lifestyle change may be tough at first, but it's well worth the sacrifice as the extra money in the bank will keep you motivated to stay the course.

The 30-day tracking exercise provides time for you to gather as much information as possible to devise your personal financial strategy. Don't cheat by restricting your daily consumption during the research period. Accurately tracking your spending habits will reveal those activities that you may need to restrict to accomplish your financial goals. However, the tracking exercise will also highlight those positive habits that you've employed, which are encouraging benchmarks for future success.

Automate Your Savings

Make saving automatic. Instead of thinking about where you're going to spend your hard-earned money, think about how much you need to save in order to take advantage of a life-changing opportunity. If you assign purpose to your money, you will keep better track of it and not lose it to random impulse spending.

Allocate a percentage of your income to your savings account using an automatic direct transfer. Set a goal for what percentage of your monthly income you will allocate to savings at the beginning of the month instead of waiting until the end of the month. If you don't assign purpose to your income early, overspending is the end result. A safe percentage of your income to start saving is between five to ten percent. The key is to learn to live below your means and progressively save more of your monthly income.

Save Extra Income

When you receive extra money—whether from a bonus, tax refund, raise, gift, or new client payment—make it a habit to put those funds directly into savings. If you've just finished paying off a loan, keep setting aside the same amount each month in your savings account. This simple habit turns temporary income boosts or freed-up cash flow into progress toward your financial goals. Another way to strengthen this practice is to set a specific purpose for the extra money, such as building your emergency fund, adding to a vacation fund, or putting it toward a down payment. Giving those dollars a clear assignment reduces the temptation to spend on impulse. Over time, consistently saving unexpected income will accelerate your progress and give you a strong financial cushion.

Create an Emergency Fund

The 10 Coin Commandments Biblical Financial System will prepare you for the random events that come up in our everyday lives that reduce savings. We are often unable to save because of unplanned events that deplete our savings. It seems like every time there is an increase in income, or just when your savings account balance is moving in the right direction, some random emergency requires you to use those funds you've worked so hard to save.

An emergency fund consists of three to six months of income in your savings account in case of an emergency such as a job loss, car trouble, sudden health issue or other unforeseen circumstances. The emergency fund is separate from your retirement or traditional savings accounts and is specifically created for emergencies only. An emergency is not for you to dip into when that new item you've been watching goes on sale.

It's understandable to have concerns about saving three to six months of income or expenses, particularly if you have substantial debt, live on a fixed income, or have unpredictable or inconsistent income. Creating an emergency fund may not seem realistic given your current financial situation. However, the emergency fund can be a work in progress with small contributions of as little as 10 dollars a month. The key is to keep working at it until you've saved enough over time. The larger the emergency fund, the better. The security of having 12 months of all household expenses covered is a level of freedom that will give you the confidence to achieve your financial goals.

Save & Rescue

"But if any provide not for his own, and specially for those of his own house, he hath denied the faith, and is worse than an infidel." – 1 Timothy 5:8

The Bible makes it a requirement that we provide for our community, and especially for those within our own house or under the same roof. Strong homes lead to strong communities. Strong communities lead to a strong society when group economics are practiced properly. When the collective society has made provisions for the community, we all benefit through economic stability.

Saving is a preventative measure; your finances serve as protection against harm or danger. In this context, a financial rescue means having the ability to either be removed from or remove yourself from a harmful situation. Cash savings act as a shield, helping you withstand financial challenges and giving you the means to leave toxic or threatening environments when necessary.

The danger you need to protect yourself from may include job loss, unforeseen medical issues, household emergencies (hot water heater, HVAC, plumbing, etc.), car servicing and repairs, unexpected travel, death-related expenses or more. Additional insurance can help with the costs of these unexpected emergencies.

Recently, my wife and I needed to replace our HVAC in the middle of summer. Our system was over ten years old, but it never gave us any problems. Coincidentally, our central air gave us issues at the most inopportune time–during a heat wave. Small fixes weren't an option, and the technician recommended a replacement of the entire system for approximately nine thousand dollars. After getting a second opinion from another company and a good friend in the business, we knew the price was reasonable, and we replaced the entire HVAC system.

We made the payment using our savings. However, home warranty protection for major systems and appliances offers another way to pay for emergency expenses. These additional insurers do not require maintenance records or inspections, nor is the age of the system or appliance a factor in determining the cost. Home warranties protect what hazard insurance does not. Some energy companies provide affordable protection plans for repairs, covered parts, and labor with the dependability of expert technicians. If your energy company does not have residential or business programs available, there are several comparable options to help with the repair and replacement of systems and appliances. At the time, our additional insurance only cost around $100.00 per month, including roof replacement.

This experience reinforced why saving—and having safeguards like insurance—matters so much. Emergencies will always come, but when you've prepared in advance, you can face them with confidence instead of fear. Savings isn't just about money—it's about protecting your family, preserving your peace, and honoring God by managing your resources wisely.

MAXIMIZING YOUR SAVINGS

Defense Wins Championships

"Wisdom is good with an inheritance: and by it there is profit to them that see the sun. For wisdom is a defence, and money is a defence: but the excellency of knowledge is, that wisdom giveth life to them that have it." – Ecclesiastes 7:11-12

At the beginning of the basketball season in high school, we all knew one thing. We would have to earn the opportunity to play offense. Training revolved heavily around playing individual on-ball defense, off-the-ball defense, team help defense, and defensive rebounding to end the possession. We were barely allowed to touch the basketball for two weeks until we learned how to play this side of the ball. We ran so much to get in shape that it felt like we were on the track team.

The primary training and strategy centered around man-to-man defense. After the coaches believed we played man-to-man well enough, we transitioned to playing every type of zone defense.

In finance, building a strong, consistent savings has always been the traditional man-to-man defense. Once you've created a budget that outlines a specific plan for saving six to twelve months of income, you will need to employ more complex strategies. Why is this important? It is important because financial flexibility helps you manage resources effectively. Risk management (defense) changes depending on the environment, with multiple factors working to help you accomplish your savings goals.

Understanding Interest Rates

There are some important factors to consider when developing your savings strategy. The first key factor is the interest rate, which is the amount of money charged to the borrower for use of the lender's money over a period of time.

The second key factor is time. When it comes to interest rates, the key factor is how long you keep your money in an interest-earning account. This will determine how your money grows. The more time, the better.

The third key factor involves the interest payments from your bank. How your bank pays you interest on your deposit is important. Most banks compound interest, which is defined as the amount the bank or financial institution pays on your initial deposit and also on the interest your deposit has earned over time. When shopping for which savings account will pay you the most, compare the annual percentage yield (APY) of the accounts. The higher the APY, the more interest income you'll receive. Know whether the interest is compounded daily, monthly, or quarterly, as it represents each time you'll be paid interest on the new total amount in your account. The more frequently your money is compounded, the more interest income you'll earn.

Compound Interest Calculation

The formula for calculating compound interest is:

$M = P(1+i)n$

- Where M is the final amount including principal.
- P is the principal amount.
- I is the rate of interest per year.
- N is the number of years invested.

If you were looking to invest $1,000.00 for three years with a compound interest of 5%, the formula calculation would read: $M = 1000 (1+5\%)3$

- Step 1: Change the 5% to 0.05
  - Equation now reads $M = 1000 (1+.05)3$

- Step 2: Add 1 and .05
  - Equation now reads $M = 1000 (1.05)3$

- Step 3: Cube 1.05 (1.05 x 1.05 x 1.05)
  - Equation now reads $M = 1000 \times 1.16$

- Step 4: Multiply 1000 by 1.16
- **Answer = $1,157.63**

The Rule of 72

The Rule of 72 is used to determine how many years it will take for your initial investment to double, given the interest rate. For instance, if you have an 8% rate of return (interest rate), divide 72 by 8 to get 9 years. This means that at 8% interest, your investment will double in nine years.

Water

"And God said, Let there be a firmament in the midst of the waters, and let it divide the waters from the waters. And God made the firmament, and divided the waters which were under the firmament from the waters which were above the firmament: and it was so. And God called the firmament Heaven. And the evening and the morning were the second day. And God said, Let the waters under the heaven be gathered together unto one place, and let the dry land appear: and it was so."
– Genesis 1:6-9

Water plays an important part in the creation of the world. The Earth and all its inhabitants could not exist without water. Water is important for biological processes, transporting nutrients in the blood and between cells. God made water above the heavens and water below the heavens. Water gives life, but is also a protective boundary that keeps us separated. Water is flexible, nurtures, sustains, protects, upholds, moves, transports, and even has the power to destroy.

We can compare cash to water: when saved, it provides life to all of your goals, flexibility in unforeseen circumstances, sustains the household, provides protection, makes paid wise counsel accessible, and allows you to take advantage of opportunities when moving money upstream or downstream to support business ventures and investments.

The **Waterfall Method** is a fascinating estate planning strategy that uses whole life insurance to efficiently build and sustain generational wealth. It is a self-perpetuating wealth cycle where families can create their own bank and borrow to build businesses, acquire real estate assets, or make other investments.

Start by setting up a trust to hold your life insurance policies. This lets you decide how the money will be used by future generations and ensures it's managed the way you want. A trust also helps avoid the probate process, can lower estate taxes, protects the money from creditors, and lets you set rules for how and when your heirs receive their inheritance—encouraging wise money management. Once the trust is set up, list your beneficiaries and take out life insurance policies for each one.

Next, choose life insurance policies that last for the person's entire life and require regular premium payments. Make sure the policy includes a cash value feature that grows over time and can be borrowed from if needed.

Finally, in addition to the death benefit that is paid when the insured passes away, as you pay your premiums, the insurance policies accumulate tax-deferred cash value from investments made by the insurance company. You can borrow against this cash value if needed—for personal use or investments—effectively serving as your own bank. Behind the scenes, the insurance company invests the premiums in things like stocks to help grow that cash value over time.

Policyholders can borrow against the cash value for needs such as home purchases, real estate investments, education, and business capital. The loan interest from the insurance company may be more favorable than traditional loans from an external bank.

The loans can be repaid with flexible terms, allowing the policyholder the ability to manage their cash flows without sacrificing other investments or savings. Upon the death of the policyholder, the death benefit, minus any outstanding loans, is passed to the beneficiaries.

The Waterfall Method preserves wealth within the family by growing the amount of wealth over generations. Advantages of this method include: (1) The cash value and death benefit are liquid savings that can support the family through a difficult time or to fund an opportunity; (2) Portfolio growth and payouts have tax advantages securing the transfer of wealth; (3) Borrowing and repaying the cash value allows families to finance their ventures without using external sources such as banks; and (4) Integrating these strategies into estate planning can streamline the transfer of wealth, avoid probate court, and reduce estate taxes.

Being your own bank allows for the control and direction of liquidity, cash flow, or currency. By definition, a bank, much like a river bank, restricts the flow of water and directs it either downstream or upstream.

Money is water. Liquid assets include cash, marketable securities (stocks, bonds, mutual funds), and money market accounts.

Just as the human body is approximately 60% water, your personal assets should ideally be 60% liquid, where you can access cash or cash equivalents quickly when needed. The same goes for your business, where liquidity includes cash, marketable securities, inventory, and accounts receivables.

It's recommended that we drink roughly 15.5 cups of water per day to stay healthy. When it comes to your personal finances, you should evaluate how much liquidity you have. Just as dehydration can harm your physical health, a lack of liquidity can put your financial well-being at risk. Having enough liquid assets ensures flexibility, stability, and sustainability—especially during times of uncertainty or volatile economic conditions.

During the COVID-19 pandemic, those with cash savings (water) or access to bank debt were able to increase earnings. Home property values dropped significantly. Private Equity Firms, Hedge Funds, and corporations with available cash purchased homes. These companies are currently renting these homes that they purchased at a discount. The firms were able to acquire properties because they had the available cash and access to cheap paper (debt) that allowed them to invest in a down market. Now, not only are rent prices high, but home values have skyrocketed.

During the same period, some individual consumers were able to take advantage of very low interest rates (between 2%-3%), acquiring homes across the country as investments for themselves. Within five years, some home values have gone up 80%. A home across the street from me sold for $515,000 during the pandemic. In five years, the house two doors down sold for $930,000. Multi-family homes in urban areas saw an explosion in value, along with increased rent prices. For owners of multi-family properties, the rising rents increased income as the property value increased. Access to cash (water) to make strategic investments in very cyclical economic environments is the key to generating wealth. Individuals now have access to equity, which can be used to acquire more investment properties or other types of investments. Increased cash flow improves the owner's standard of living and allows for strategic investments in income-producing assets.

Offers from buyers purchasing properties with cash get priority; they pay less in closing costs, can close on the home much quicker than buyers requiring financing, and have more buying power when negotiating price. Drink more water!

STAYING THE COURSE

The hardest part about saving is sticking to the savings plan. As soon as you create a savings plan and assign purpose to accomplish your goals, your friends will ask you to come hang out for drinks or dinner, go on vacation, or even ask for financial assistance. Figure out a tactful way to say NO. Building a savings and emergency fund is impossible if the answer is always yes. Find a list of free things to do, or invite your friends over instead of going out to save money. A great habit is to create a fun fund where you are allocating money toward vacations, eating out, parties, and entertainment. This way, if the fun fund has been used up for the month, you know the answer is "no" to any more fun. On the bright side, if the fun fund was not used, it continues to grow, awaiting the next opportunity for a good time.

Retail Sales Traps

If a store item has an original price of $100.00 with a sale price that is 50% off, how much did you save? The answer is ZERO! If you purchase an item that's 50% off, you haven't saved a dime; you've just spent less. The excitement of finding a deal may be enticing, especially if it's on something you've been eying for a while. However, you can't spend and save at the same time. Either you're spending or you're saving.

The COVID-19 pandemic caused the retail industry to lose billions due to the lack of in-store customers. The shift to e-commerce had already begun as families began to spend most of their money shopping online for convenience. Lockdowns of non-essential businesses meant that governments put even further strain on retail businesses. Restaurants that survived on foot traffic from the employees of corporations and large businesses suffered as people worked from home.

The recession caused by the pandemic changed customer spending, making families more fiscally conservative. The retail industry had very little choice but to bombard consumers with sales of 65%, 75%, and even 80% off. Of course, I purchased items for 80% off, and you would be insane to forfeit such an opportunity if your family had some financial stability. The point is not to let the sale derail you from your financial plan and savings goals. As the scripture's instruction states, it's better to save a portion of seven to eight times your income, for we know not what evil shall be upon the earth.

Partner for Growth and Accountability

There's a saying, "If you want to go fast, go by yourself, but if you want to go far, go together." Household savings goals allow you and your partner to grow closer together, communicate consistently about what it will take to achieve your family goals, and create opportunities for accountability if someone gets off track.

When entering into a relationship, the most consistent advice from counselors and married couples is to communicate. The problem is, no one tells you what to actually communicate about. As a result, you end up having meaningless surface-level conversations that end in arguments. Money tends to be at the center of at least one of those recurring arguments between couples.

You need to discuss savings goals with your partner for accountability and support. Creating and accomplishing goals together will actually bring you closer and make your bond stronger.

Whether you are the spender and your spouse the saver, or vice versa, discussing how you plan to reach your savings goals is a vital part of a healthy, mature relationship. You may choose to use a joint bank account where both of you agree to contribute a specific amount each month. Alternatively, you can work together using your individual savings accounts. No matter how you create your plan, communicate with your partner regularly about your savings and money goals, and hold each other accountable.

Expect some of these conversations to be difficult at times. However, it's impossible to solve any problem, especially about money, by avoiding the issue. Learn to have difficult conversations.

Peniaphobia

Peniaphobia is an irrational fear or anxiety regarding poverty or the risk of becoming poor.

Don't be afraid to be broke. A capitalist society conditions you to believe and often actively participate, through peer pressure and ostracization, in negative feelings or behaviors toward the poor. Being poor and being broke are two different phenomena. Being broke means not having money right now or excess disposable cash in the short term. Being poor is an ongoing inability to generate sufficient income required to live at a standard that is considered to be normal in society. The mentality is consistent with the belief that opportunities are limited because they are allocated, not created, success can't be replicated, and the inability to think through long-term benefits versus instant gratification.

Sometimes, a person with a net worth of over $1 million is still broke. The reason one's current financial condition may make them feel broke varies. If someone has acquired depreciating non-income-producing assets to impress others by appearing to live an excessive lifestyle, they will eventually end up poor. However, if someone sacrifices to invest in income producing assets or investments that generate passive income while living a prudent lifestyle until their financial win, they may feel broke.

It's important to get comfortable with being broke from time to time. Once money is deployed, you may feel broke waiting on the return on your investment. If you are uncomfortable being broke at times, you may miss out on opportunities. This does not mean put your hard-earned money at significant risk and skip the due diligence process. It means you need to save money to wisely invest your hard-earned money.

Commandment V
Credit & Debt Management

"For the LORD thy God blesseth thee, as he promised thee: and thou shalt lend unto many nations, but thou shalt not borrow; and thou shalt reign over many nations, but they shall not reign over thee." – Deuteronomy 15:6

A S GOD FULFILLS HIS PROMISE with blessings free from sorrow, the verse reminds us to take a position of power and authority as a lender instead of living in debt. It is through debt that people find themselves in servitude.

The use of debt is heavily debated. Some advise that you avoid it at all costs, while others believe that using other people's money is the primary way to create wealth, grow your business, or purchase a home. Credit and debt play an important role in society, where the relationship between the borrower and lender, if functional, can lead to economic growth, or, if dysfunctional, result in an economic depression. When banks are hesitant to lend, businesses that rely on loans for day-to-day operations or growth may struggle to access the cash they need—and without enough liquidity, they risk going out of business.

Now think of yourself as a business. What would happen if you were personally over-reliant on debt through credit cards or other forms of debt with limited cash or other liquid assets? It would be extremely difficult to navigate through the challenges of an economic downturn, loss of income, or rise in inflation.

Is all debt bad? No–if used responsibly for business purposes, it can generate significant amounts of income and create wealth. However, when it is used strictly for consumption, it can lead to bankruptcy and what some Bible verses would call "slavery."

Lending can be a highly profitable business. Banks earn income by charging interest rates based on the risk profile of the borrower. The higher the risk, the higher the interest rate, and the more the bank stands to earn. As a result, it is extremely important to understand and manage debt, as the cost is so much greater for borrowers with a poor credit profile. An inability to pay off your debt comes with a cost. Debt, if used at all, should be temporary and focused on acquiring an income-producing asset.

The position in the Bible is clear. The lender holds the position of power, while the borrower is in a dependent role, making debt feel like a form of financial bondage. God does not want you in bondage, which is why we're instructed to lend but not borrow.

How can we possibly avoid getting into debt, given our culture of consumption and excess? Depending on your geographical location, particularly in the Northeast and on the West Coast, it's very difficult to obtain a living wage or stay afloat, given the cost of living. It becomes even more difficult if you live in a one-income household. Yet, living below your means and choosing to live debt-free is the beginning of becoming financially free.

REASONS FOR USING CREDIT

People use credit for many reasons, including:

- Buying something today and paying it back over time instead of waiting.
- Having the flexibility to cover major purchases like a computer, car, or college tuition when cash isn't available.
- Enjoying safer transactions—especially online—thanks to fraud protection policies.
- Making it easier to rent an apartment or qualify for a mortgage when paying cash isn't realistic.
- Securing a loan to start or expand a business.

Whatever the reason, your available credit and reputation for handling debt are critical to your future financial success. Even if you don't plan on using debt, this information, provided to lenders by credit reporting agencies through a FICO Score and credit report, will determine the cost of all financial products and services.

FICO SCORE

No matter what anyone tells you, a high credit score does not mean you are rich or will become wealthy. A FICO Score is a tool used by lenders to determine the probability of repayment based on your previous borrowing activity. It is only a tool that will help you accomplish some of your financial goals. Having an excellent FICO score is the beginning of putting yourself in position for financial success. A magical key to riches will not be handed out once you've achieved an excellent credit rating. However, the financial habits that have resulted in an excellent credit score are the building blocks of wealth creation. An excellent FICO Score will allow you access to bank capital, give you bargaining power when negotiating fees and other costs related to doing business, lower the amount of interest paid on loans, help with employment opportunities, and grant you access to financial planning and wealth creation strategies. An excellent score is only the beginning and must be guarded and maintained.

A FICO Score is derived using the collection of credit information on your credit report. This credit data is grouped into five categories that determine your score.

- **Payment History** accounts for 35%.
- **Current Balances (Amounts Owed)** account for 30%.
- **Length of Credit History (Credit History)** accounts for 15%.
- **New Credit** accounts for 10%.
- **Credit Diversity** accounts for the final 10% of your score.

The percentages reflect each category's level of importance in determining your FICO Score. However, there can be determining factors, particularly for those who have very little credit history, that impact a FICO score more significantly or differently, since these percentages of importance are reflective of the general population.

1. Payment History

The data for payment history reflected in your FICO Score is taken from credit payment information for specific types of accounts, which include: credit cards, retail accounts, installment loans, car loans, student loans, finance company accounts, mortgages, etc. The presence of any adverse information regarding bankruptcy, judgments, lawsuits, liens, accounts in collections, past due payments, and minimum payments affects your score. The credit data retrieved to calculate this portion of your score also considers the frequency with which you pay, the number of accounts that are being paid on time, and the number of accounts past due.

2. Amounts Owed

The amount owed data from your credit report is used to rate your reliability based on usage. As an example, you should only use between 30%-50% of your available balance on a credit card. If you have a $1,000.00 credit card limit, the most you should utilize is $500.00. Once you've gone beyond a utilization of 50% your FICO Score will be negatively impacted. Therefore, you need to use between 30%-50% and pay it down to zero. The bank will then consider you a responsible borrower and automatically increase your balance to $1,500.00. Repeat this utilization technique, and you will soon have a credit card availability of $5,000.00. Be patient, the road to wealth creation and access to bank capital is not a sprint.

3. Length of Credit History

The credit report shows when your consumer account was opened, how long each consumer account has been open, the different types of accounts that have been open for an extended period of time, and the length of time since recent account activity, including payments. Successfully managing a diverse number of consumer accounts for a number of years improves your FICO Score.

4. **New Credit**

Your credit report tracks the number of accounts recently opened and the percentage of recently opened accounts compared to those that have been open for a number of years. The number of credit inquiries with different financial institutions or potential creditors has an adverse impact on your FICO score. If there is a loan or product you want to finance, make sure you've done the research, are confident in the product, and understand all of the financing options available. You should have discussions with different lenders about pricing, interest rates, and fees charged prior to a credit pull. Before giving a lender consent to pull your credit report, negotiate fees and interest and continue to inquire about the lender's products and services based on your projected FICO score. Signing up for services that allow you access to your personal credit score helps with the negotiations. It is important to track your score on a monthly basis for any changes or possible fraud. When you give lenders permission to pull your credit, make sure, particularly if there are multiple inquiries from different lenders, that all credit inquiries are done within the same month (30 days). Credit inquiries have an adverse impact on your credit score, but only for 30 days. After 30 days from your last inquiry, your score goes back up. Therefore, only have your credit pulled within that 30-day time frame, regardless of the number of inquiries. What you don't want is to have your credit pulled every month and your score continue to go down every 30 days due to multiple inquiries. The best approach is to compare the top three lenders providing the most advantageous products and services. Then decide on the one that best fits your needs, having your credit pulled only once.

5. Credit Diversity

Lenders want to see that you are able to successfully manage different types of credit products, including credit cards, mortgages, retail accounts, auto loans, and other consumer finance accounts. The ability to responsibly manage multiple types of credit products improves your score.

A FICO Score takes into consideration all five categories of information, not just one or two. No one piece of information or one category alone will determine your score. The importance of any factor will depend on the overall information from your credit report. For some, a given factor may be more important than for someone else with a different credit history. In addition, as the information in your credit report changes, so does the importance of any given factor in determining your FICO Score. As a result, it's difficult to ascertain how important any single category is in determining your score, as even the levels of importance are reflective of the general population and will be different depending on the individual credit profile. What you must pay close attention to is the mix of information used to determine your credit score, which varies from person to person and for any one person over a period of time.

A FICO Score is only reflective of the information on your credit report. Lenders make credit decisions based on a number of factors, including your income, how long you've worked at your current place of employment or have been self-employed, and what type of credit you are requesting.

A FICO Score considers both positive and negative information from your credit report. Late payments will lower your score, but establishing a good track record of making payments on time will raise your score as those negative marks fall off the report.

What's not in your FICO Score?

A credit report has a lot of your personal financial information in it. However, due to regulatory guidelines, certain personal attributes are excluded in order to comply with fair lending laws and guidelines. Therefore, a credit reporting system will not include race, color, religion, national origin, sex, or marital status as a factor in generating your score or in lenders rendering a credit decision. U.S. laws prohibit credit scoring systems from considering these factors, as well as any receipt of public assistance, or any information regarding an exercise of consumer rights under the Consumer Credit Protection Act. Though your birthdate is on the credit report, the actual FICO score does not take into consideration age.

As mentioned, a lender will use other factors, such as income or the length of time in your current job, to render a credit decision in addition to your FICO Score. However, the FICO Score itself does not consider a person's salary, occupation, title, employer, date employed or employment history.

Banks are also regulated and required to make sure they aren't accepting deposits from urban neighborhoods and declining to lend in those same neighborhoods where they are receiving deposits. Financial institutions were known for taking deposits from minorities, declining loan requests from these same groups, and lending in areas outside of the deposit community. As a result, there have been regulations that require financial institutions to document every aspect of the loan request process, including personal demographics, if the client is willing to provide them. This will allow for a comparison of applicants who have the same profession and incomes to determine if there is discrimination in the banks, or lenders, credit approval or in interest charged. Bottom line, where you live is not factored into your FICO Score.

Trades on your credit report do not show the annual percentage rate for each loan, and rate information does not impact your credit score. Each lender must price the loan based on their independent review of your credit profile. This is to prevent collusion where banks can overcharge clients by issuing higher interest rates, which would limit competition and the ability to find suitable substitutes or replacements for fair loan products.

When you check your own credit report to monitor your credit, it's considered a consumer-initiated inquiry and does not impact your FICO Score. In addition, promotional inquiries by potential lenders looking to market their business do not adversely impact your FICO Score. Your FICO Score does not include any information that hasn't been proven to predict future credit performance, including participation in credit counseling.

How Does Credit Scoring Help You?

The credit scoring system was created to make it easier for both the customer and lender to make decisions regarding products and provide some symmetry within the lending community on how to process requests for credit. The credit score attempts to give lenders a fast and objective measure of your personal credit risk. It is designed to be a consistent metric that looks to eliminate a slow, archaic manual process that has historically been inconsistent and biased.

A credit score can be delivered instantaneously, allowing for verification of your personal information and expediting the credit review and approval process for most retail products and services. Many retail credit decisions can be made within minutes, depending on the lender's policies and procedures, including mortgage pre-approvals. The score is reflective of an individual customer's willingness and ability to repay debt. Most lenders have a minimum credit score requirement.

An efficient credit decision process is better than dragging someone through an extensive process that renders the same decision. A streamlined credit process saves time, money, and eliminates frustration.

Another benefit of having a credit scoring system is speed to market for customers who shop online. The consumer transition from brick-and-mortar retail shopping to buying most of their products online led to the most profitable Cyber Monday in U.S. history and is reflective of our preferences for convenience. Online banking and the ability to apply for loans to purchase products from your favorite retail stores have made personal credit scores that much more important.

With the credit scoring system, lenders can focus on the facts related to credit risk instead of personal feelings about the applicant. Using a system that restricts bias based on protected categories makes the credit approval process fairer.

In addition, having a reporting system where past delinquencies and poor performance will not remain on a personal credit file forever is important and allows the individual the opportunity to grow past earlier mistakes. Previous credit mistakes fade as time passes and recent payment patterns report good standings. More significant items like bankruptcy, judgments, foreclosures, collection accounts, and adverse public information will remain on a personal credit report for seven years. As stated in Deuteronomy 15:1, *"At the end of every seven years thou shalt make a release."*

Lenders who use credit scoring can approve more loans as credit scoring provides precise criteria on which to base credit decisions. It allows lenders the ability to identify individuals who are likely to perform well in the future despite any previous issues showing on the credit report. Credit scores give the lender confidence in extending credit, as they have access to your full report and risk metrics that assist in making credit decisions.

An automated credit process, which includes the credit scoring system, makes the lending process more efficient and less costly for lenders, who in turn pass on those savings to customers.

PERSONAL CREDIT ASSESSMENT

The process of using credit to your advantage begins with an evaluation of your current credit profile. To start, print your credit report with the FICO Score, monthly budget, and bank statements. In conducting your personal credit assessment, you need to ask the following:

- Are you managing your checking and savings accounts well, never spending more than what's in the account? Overdraft fees are not only costly but also indicative of your inability to manage your monthly income and expenses. A monthly forecast of income and expenses helps assign purpose to the money you're projected to earn. A daily review of your accounts and a weekly review of your budget will give you time to make adjustments and help execute your financial plan. If you're not checking your banking and investment accounts daily, it will be difficult to achieve your daily, weekly, and monthly financial goals.
- Are all of your bills paid on time? Responsible debt management of all bills is essential to establishing and maintaining good credit. If you have any issues making payments, contact the company and work out an arrangement with them directly.
- Are you spending more than you make? Purchasing an item prior to receiving income leads to debt and income mismanagement. If you don't have six months of income saved, an emergency fund, or retirement investments, consumer purchases should not be a priority. It's important to plan your big purchases. However, if the purchase is not in line with your saving and investing strategy, it inhibits your long-term financial success. Address your behavior and change it.
- Are you paying less than 10% of your monthly income on credit card debt? Is your total debt less than 20% of your annual net income? The standard rule is to never borrow more than 20% of your annual net income.

Signs of Good Credit

Determine where you are in the journey of establishing exceptional credit and apply the appropriate strategies to achieve this goal. I go into more detail regarding the specific strategies later in the chapter. If you're making much more than the minimum payment on credit cards, paying your bills on time, never missing a payment, borrowing well below your credit limit, or have paid off all of your consumer debt obligations, it's a good sign that you have established good credit. As a result, it will be easier to borrow money, avoid fees for late payments, and save money on interest.

Signs of Bad Credit

Signs that you have bad credit include behaviors such as:

- Paying below the minimum on your credit card
- Paying bills late
- Charging over your credit limit
- Having too much debt
- Taking 60 to 90 days to cover bills that should be paid monthly
- Juggling payments between creditors to keep them satisfied
- Having a consistently overdrawn checking account
- Bouncing checks and scrambling to make deposits
- Having difficulty covering monthly bills and expenses due to any reduction in income or an unusual expense
- Keeping credit card balances at their maximum limits, with these balances remaining the same or increasing over time
- Paying off credit card charges you made over a year ago
- Fighting with family over expenses and ignoring the phone

These are all signs of debt issues. Having bad credit means you're going to have a difficult time borrowing money. If approved for a loan, you will spend a lot of money on interest. You've likely paid late fees on past due payments, and the cost of doing business has increased, given your negative reputation regarding repayment.

Improving Your FICO Score

Understanding what factors affect your credit score helps with creating a strategy to continually improve it. While some are chasing the elusive perfect score of 850, the key is to actively find ways to improve your credit profile and avoid the traps that lower your credit score.

The easiest way to improve your credit score is to pay all your obligations and bills on time. Delinquent payments and collections have a severely negative impact on your FICO Score. If you've missed payments, you must get current on your debt obligations and stay current. Those current payments will move the past due payments off your credit report and improve your score.

Paying off a collection account will not improve your credit score. If you can, call the initial owner of the trade or obligation and negotiate getting this off your credit report, then pay. However, if the lender does not agree to provide a written notice that they will no longer report the trade as a collection account on your credit report, do not pay. The collection companies will take your payment and then sell your personal information to the next collection company who will then ask for the same payment which will never come off your credit report. If the collection account is an error, or has been paid up to date with proof of payment, you need to contact the three credit reporting agencies and dispute the information. If the collection account information is accurate, you should wait seven years until the collection status falls off the report.

If it becomes difficult for you to uphold your financial obligations, contact the creditors directly and ask for help. They may close the account and place you on a program with lower payments, where you will at least be able to maintain your credit score. Once back on your feet, you can resume the normal payments.

Another way to improve your credit score is to maintain outstanding balances equal to or less than 30% - 50% of the limit on all credit cards. As previously mentioned, high utilization lowers your credit score. In addition to maintaining low balances on credit card debt, pay off as much debt as possible while keeping the credit lines open. Do not close the accounts, as doing so will reduce your credit availability and lower your credit score. The exception is if the card has an annual fee. In that case, you should close the account, as there are many credit products available that do not require an annual fee.

Do not open up several credit lines at once just to increase your credit availability. I advise you to open new accounts gradually. Opening a number of new credit cards all at once will only hurt your score and your ability to take advantage of 0% promotional interest rates, which can be extended over a significant period if done strategically.

If you've had credit trouble and want to improve your score, open one credit card and pay the balance off in full every month.

Do not spend more than you have allocated for full repayment. If the card limit is $500, charge $250 on the card and pay the entire balance off within the billing cycle so that you will not be charged interest. This will help to re-establish your credit and improve your score. As your credit availability for this card grows from $500 to $1,000, use 40% to 50% ($500) and pay it off at the end of the month. You don't have to borrow each month. However, consistent and responsible usage of debt will continue to increase your availability and improve your credit score.

As mentioned, a diverse credit mix shows your ability to responsibly manage multiple forms of debt. Therefore, your credit score improves as you continue to manage different types of credit obligations. However, this does not mean you need to find different types of loans to apply for to improve your score. This is not a reason to get into debt. The intent is to obtain an exceptional credit score and then move from using debt to cash or a debit card. The end goal is to have no consumer debt at all.

EXECUTE THE PLAN

After performing an assessment of your credit profile, the next step is to create a plan to improve your FICO score and overall credit profile. The plan must revolve around those five categories that impact your credit score. Everyone's financial situation is different, so work to improve your score by setting reasonable goals and timelines for each category that needs the most improvement.

Make sure you ask for help. Every city in the country has a nonprofit organization with debt counseling centers that provide advice free of charge. Contact the Consumer Credit Counseling Service in your area, or contact your lender, who should also have information on the nonprofit organizations that assist in debt management. Use a budget to create a plan of action and track your progress. Don't give up! Cut up your credit cards and pay the balances down to zero; do not close the accounts. There are also a few strategies that will help improve your score rather quickly.

Debt Snowball Payoff Strategy

The debt snowball method is a debt reduction strategy where you list your loan balances from smallest to largest. On those large balances, make the minimum payment. On the smallest balance, pay as much as possible until you pay off that debt. As the loan with the smallest balance is paid off, you will gain a sense of accomplishment and renewed energy to move on to the next smallest balance.

As mentioned, paying the minimum on your credit cards will lower your credit score. Therefore, I would suggest paying a little more than the minimum on a credit card if possible. If you persist in paying off your loan balances and incur no additional debt, your financial situation and score will improve, but most importantly, you will be eliminating debt.

Credit Card Hustle

Most banks offer several types of credit cards that provide various rewards. These often include an introductory 0% APR, 0% introductory interest rate on balance transfers with a transfer fee and no annual fee. The introductory period is usually between 12-23 months. The bank anticipates that you will take advantage of the low introductory 0% APR but will not pay off the balance in full by the end of the period. The APR after the 12-23-month introductory period is usually between 12% - 24% depending on your creditworthiness. It's a form of entrapment intended to entice a customer to enter into a cycle of debt, or slavery, as the Bible suggests. Implement the plan below once you've reached a FICO score of 650 or above. The intention is to use the banks 0% APR introductory period to gain access to free money and high credit availability while increasing your credit score.

How It Works:

Step 1- Apply for a credit card from a major provider that offers a 0% introductory APR. Accept the highest credit limit you're approved for, and use the interest-free period and any balance transfer offers strategically. The goal is to pay off the entire balance before the introductory period ends, so when the regular interest rate kicks in, it won't affect you. This way, you've essentially borrowed money without paying interest.

Step 2- Do not close the original account. The key to increasing your credit score is having access to multiple sources of credit and showing you are capable of properly managing the debt; the more credit availability, the better.

Step 3- Apply for the same credit card with the same bank once the introductory period has ended. If the exact credit card isn't available, the bank will offer several others with a 0% introductory period, a 0% balance transfer period, no annual fee and no balance transfer fee. Look to get the same or higher credit limit with the new credit card.

Step 4- Make sure that the credit card is completely paid off by the end of the introductory period. To protect your FICO score and avoid carrying debt after the introductory period, try to use no more than half of your credit limit. Most importantly, be sure to pay off the entire balance before the promotional period ends.

Step 5- Do not close the new account. This will decrease the credit availability you have and adversely impact your credit score.

Step 6- Consolidate both credit cards. Though you are in effect closing an account, you are not decreasing your credit exposure or credit availability. If the first card was a $10k credit card and the second credit card is a $10k credit card, consolidate both cards into the credit card that has the lowest interest rate. The new $20k consolidated credit card will have zero balance. The individual credit card availability did not change, so your FICO score will not change either. Do not use this card. The introductory period has passed, and the temptation to use the new $20k availability will be great. The point is to use free money, incur no fees or interest, and build your credit FICO score.

Step 7- Apply for a credit card with another bank, requesting the new consolidated credit card availability amount. In this example, the requested amount would be $20k. Apply for a 0% introductory interest rate and 0%

balance transfer no-fee credit card. Use the free money, making sure you've paid off the balance in full by the time the introductory 12-23-month period is complete.

Step 8- Do not close the credit card.

Step 9- Apply for the same credit card with the same bank for $20k to take advantage of the 0% introductory APR and the 0% balance transfer with no annual fee. Use the free money, and pay the balance off completely within the introductory period. Be careful not to succumb to the temptation of buying extravagant items or charging items that will create a balance you cannot pay off at the end of the introductory period. Do not fall into the trap. Pay off the entire balance at the end of the introductory period.

Step 10- Do not close the accounts.

Step 11- Consolidate the two accounts into one $40k credit card account. The credit availability has not decreased; you've just decreased the amount of plastic in your wallet. You now have a $40k credit card and a $20K credit card. Your FICO score has improved drastically. You have $60k in credit availability and zero debt using free money. It's now time to move on to the next bank.

After the third bank, you can decide if you want to continue playing the game or not. You will likely have over $100k in credit availability, zero debt, a very low post-introductory APR of 7% compared to the 16%-24% of the first card, and banks will be begging for your business.

The additional liquidity will also help if you're looking to eventually start your own business. The strategy does not take the place of an extensive savings plan, an emergency fund, or a 401(k) retirement plan. The purpose of employing the strategy is to gain access to bank credit for free, even if only for 23 months, and build your credit profile. If you reach a point where you need to apply for long-term debt, you will have a credit history of managing $100k to support the request. Make sure you also have the income to support the monthly payments if you decide a term loan is best.

This strategy only works if you have self-restraint and financial discipline. The Credit Card Hustle is intended to help streamline the wealth creation cycle by creating access to credit that can be a source of liquidity. The available liquidity created from using the Credit Card Hustle strategy puts you in a position to take advantage of wealth creation opportunities at a zero percent introductory rate for up to 23 months. Imagine having access to an extra $100k of free money to be used for a well-researched and solid investment opportunity that you know will be paid back within six to ten months. If the introductory period for the 0% interest rate is approaching and there is a balance, go to your local bank and get a small personal loan with a low fixed rate to pay off the balance. Could you do a balance transfer to another credit card with a 0% rate to keep the free money game going and buy you some more time? Yes, just be careful in devising an appropriate exit strategy before you even begin the endeavor. The last thing you want is to have a $100k bill at 18% interest.

In the past, people would use a Home Equity Line of Credit (HELOC), which is much safer if you own a home with equity. This is a potentially much cheaper means of gaining access to credit, but your home will be used as collateral for the loan should there be an issue regarding repayment.

This strategy may work well for someone early in their wealth-building journey who needs quick access to cash for an opportunity. However, more experienced and high-net-worth individuals often move to more traditional financing options— like a revolving line of credit that's secured by marketable securities in a brokerage account. These types of loans typically offer low interest rates (often around 2.5%), interest-only monthly payments, and a final lump sum, or "balloon," payment when the loan term ends. Don't take a risky bet and misuse the available credit card debt and never make it to this point in your journey.

Do not Co-sign

"Be not thou one of them that strike hands, or of them that are surities for debts. If thou hast nothing to pay, why should he take away thy bed from under thee?" – Proverbs 22:26-27

The Word specifically instructs you NOT to provide a guarantee or co-sign for another person's debt by asking why you should provide surety for someone who is both unqualified and unable to repay their debts. A person should not put themselves in a position where their home (bed) can be taken from them as a result of someone else's inability to satisfy their obligations.

Once you've obtained an exceptional credit profile, maintain it at all costs. This means using credit monitoring services and making good decisions. The Bible speaks to the decision to become a cosigner on a loan. Realistically, if the person doesn't qualify and can't afford to pay off the loan, they shouldn't proceed. Being a co-signer is not a smart thing to do unless you are willing and prepared to pay off the loan if the other co-borrower is unable to do so. If not, you risk ruining that credit profile you've worked so hard to build.

LENDER VS BORROWER REAFFIRMATION

"The LORD shall open unto thee his good treasure, the heaven to give the rain unto thy land in his season, and to bless all the work of thine hand: and thou shalt lend unto many nations, and thou shalt not borrow." – Deuteronomy 28:12

The Bible is clear. The goal is to one day be in the position of a competent lender or investor and not a borrower. Even after you've successfully managed your credit profile and have zero consumer debt, you will be tempted to venture back into servitude. Resist it at all costs. Credit cards offer points and other rewards that entice you to use debt. Unless you are able to pay off the entire outstanding balance within the same billing cycle, avoid using debt. God will bless you financially and open up his good treasure, blessing the work of your hands. God then instructs you to use these blessings to lend and not borrow. This means God wants you in a position of power and prosperity, not servitude.

> *"The rich ruleth over the poor, and the borrower*
> *is servant to the lender." – Proverbs 22:7*

After reading this Bible verse, you may be in denial and unwilling to accept the truth of the statement. Accept that it is all true. This dynamic plays out not just in personal finances but across society, where governments are often influenced by wealthy individuals and special interest groups who fund political campaigns in return for policies that serve their interests. Even judges, who are meant to be impartial, are typically appointed by those same political powers. Accepting this reality is the first step toward understanding how deeply financial systems shape power and control.

The borrower is described as a servant, but the appropriate interpretation is "slave to the lender." It's apparent that we've become so comfortable with overconsumption, minimal savings, no emergency fund, and inadequate retirement that financial slavery doesn't seem all that bad. Most of us are quite oblivious to our financial perdition and contentedly travel down the road of servitude. Personal debt should be taken very seriously.

Commandment VI
Wise Counsel

*"Without counsel purposes are disappointed:
but in the multitude of counsellors they are
established (succeed)."* – Proverbs 15:22

THE VERSE EXPLAINS HOW IMPORTANT it is to have counsel, mentors, peers, friends, and family who can provide sound advice. Success is never accomplished on your own. The Bible instructs you to enlist the advice of multiple people to gain a balanced and complete perspective.

To build effective and productive long-lasting relationships, you must first establish a strong identity and purpose within yourself. A self-aware, purposeful, and independent person should create valuable connections to build diverse relationships where ideas, information, and wisdom are shared. Leaning on others' experiences and expertise through relationships with people of various professions and backgrounds puts you in the best position to achieve great success. A superior network will greatly improve your success in life, especially when it comes to achieving your financial goals. To build meaningful relationships, you will have to take the initiative to go outside of your comfort zone to get to know people you may have assumed had less in common.

The relationships you build should be genuine and organic. The challenge lies in nurturing these relationships into a strong, intellectually diverse network that advocates for you in your absence and shares timely information and opportunities that align with your financial goals. Out of habit, we tend to commune with like-minded individuals who share similar interests or are within the same profession. Everyone you meet offers an opportunity to build a mutually respectful and beneficial relationship. God puts us in a position to fulfill our purpose and live out our dreams. Don't mistake powerful relationship opportunities for mere coincidence. Seize every moment. God put us in one another's lives to grow and be a blessing.

Learn what's important to the person you're building a relationship with and figure out how you can help. Understand what aspects of the relationship they consider to be valuable. Take interest, and remember specific things about the person. Be engaged and consistent with your interaction, whether it be a frequent phone call, text message, or email. Make sure you honor your commitments, as personal actions that match your expectations build personal integrity.

While you are being purposeful in getting to know people, it's important to only build relationships with people you are willing to invest in. Healthy relationships require effort to nurture, develop, and maintain them over a period of time. Such efforts take time and should not be wasted on the wrong people. Realistically, some relationships may be more beneficial than others. However, if the person adds value, there is a significant benefit to including them in a strong personal network.

FINANCIAL ADVISORS AND MENTORS

The most valuable relationships for gaining wise financial counsel are those with professionals like bankers, financial advisors and planners, wealth managers, real estate and insurance brokers, attorneys, business owners, and experienced investors.

Bankers should have a thorough understanding of all the products and services provided by the bank to help you accomplish your various financial goals. Bankers answer and submit requests for credit, manage client accounts, handle client complaints, and suggest specialty products tailored to your current financial situation and level of financial sophistication.

Financial advisors are licensed professionals who are legally required to act in your best interest when helping you manage and grow your money. This is known as acting as a *fiduciary*, which means they must prioritize your needs over their own potential profit. Many advisors hold specific licenses—like the Series 7, which allows them to help you buy and sell a wide range of investments such as stocks, bonds, mutual funds, and ETFs. Other licenses, like the Series 63, 65, or 66, give them the ability to offer services and investment advice in different states. In simple terms, these licenses show that the advisor has met certain education and ethics standards to guide you responsibly on your financial journey.

Financial planners are employed to create a plan to help their clients reach long-term financial goals. Financial planners provide a broad range of financial advice but may also specialize in investments, retirement, and estate planning. When seeking a financial planner, make sure the person has a history of helping clients achieve the specific financial goals you're looking to accomplish.

Wealth management advisors are similar to financial advisors, but their advisory services are specific to high-net-worth and ultra-high-net-worth individuals and families. Wealth management incorporates structuring and planning for the purpose of growing, preserving, and protecting wealth. Wealth management strategies include estate planning, business succession, and stock-option planning.

Financial brokers help you buy and sell investments like stocks and mutual funds. Since everyday people can't trade directly on the stock market, brokers act as the middlemen between you and the exchange. Some brokers also offer tools, apps, and research to help you make smarter investment decisions. For example, beginner-friendly platforms like Charles Schwab (formerly TD Ameritrade) make it easier to trade and track your investments on your phone.

Real estate agents and brokers have similar roles when it comes to helping people buy and sell property, but they differ in how they operate and earn income. Both are licensed professionals, but while agents usually work under a broker, brokers can work independently and also manage teams of agents. Agents earn a commission when a sale closes, while brokers earn their own commission and may also receive a portion of the sales made by the agents they supervise. Whether you're buying a home, selling a property, or looking for investment opportunities, a licensed real estate professional can provide valuable guidance and access to listings, market trends, and properties that may not be widely advertised.

Licensed insurance professionals provide a list of products to protect you and your assets, but they can also be a strategy for creating and passing on wealth. Independent insurance agents provide advice on insurance products that fit your lifestyle and work with a variety of insurance companies with different coverage options to fit your individual, business, and family needs.

Business owners and investors have experience in structuring deals and running profitable businesses. They have strong relationships with banks and have access to alternative financing options. Business owners and investors will tell you what works and put you in the best situation to succeed. They'll also candidly share their mistakes and point out any ambitions you may have that are unrealistic.

Attorneys in business, wealth management, securities, and real estate are pivotal to your future success. An attorney will help you choose the proper business structure when creating your company, reduce exposure to lawsuits, draft business contracts with counterparties, protect your physical and intellectual property, and review all the terms, contracts and business agreements.

Distant relationships, which consist of individuals who are generally isolated from one another, provide new information, a different set of contacts with financial expertise, unique perspectives given their different backgrounds or professions, and insight into future money-making opportunities. Distant relationships are characterized as people you know who you don't see very often and aren't as familiar with. They may be a member of the same organization, a colleague, or even a friend of a friend. Though you may not have consistent interaction, these individuals may have access to financial information that will be the most useful in pursuit of your financial goals. The goal is to cultivate those distant relationships and structure an effective social network where diverse financial information is shared and doesn't overlap to help you accomplish your financial goals.

People you know the least may, in fact, be better positioned to help you the most. Valuable information tends to be passed within a group versus between various groups. Information within your inner circle tends to be redundant since everyone within this particular group knows one another. If your parents and close friends discuss various financial topics and help one another by sharing financial experiences, which many do not, everyone in the circle's financial position improves, but may be relatively the same. However, if there is useful strategic financial information that an acquaintance possesses, this information is likely to be new and unique. Financial information with the greatest potential value is likely to be held by those you aren't very familiar with, and maybe specific, exclusive, and most importantly, non-redundant. Be sure to gain access to both your inner family circle and grow an outside network.

This network can be fairly large and should consist of bankers, lenders, entrepreneurs, local politicians, local not-for-profits that may provide grants and loans, real estate developers, university business professors, and urban and regional planning directors. This network provides the best opportunity to take advantage of timely information that will put you in a position to make money. The key is to make them familiar with your goals and interests so that those within the network think of you when they get new information, encounter someone who will be helpful in accomplishing your goals and are able to get you in front of decision makers.

An efficient network provides expanded access to information and ideas, increased speed and timing in receiving pertinent financial information, and more referrals by those within your greater network, which is a competitive advantage, facilitating your ability to get the right financial information at the right time.

Strong relationships are where there is a strong bond and consistent communication between both family and non-family members. Those relationships are with people you've known for a significant amount of time, are comfortable sharing personal experiences, and trust their perspective, even if you don't always agree. The high level of frequency and familiarity in strong relationships is beneficial because they will likely be the most transparent and supportive when you need assistance and help to push your financial agenda. Individuals in a close network will stick together and are very supportive, making it easier to ask for assistance in locating financial professionals. It is also an opportunity to leverage their experience regarding financial matters.

The collection of people strategically placed within your various networks has implications for how successful you will be. Use strong relationships as a sounding board for your financial aspirations and ask for contacts and references of individuals they believe will help. A strong network of family and friends can be invaluable when working toward your financial goals, since they're more likely to share honest experiences about what has worked—and what hasn't.

In the book *Black Faces in White Places* by Randal Pinkett and Jeffrey Robinson, the authors introduce the concept of a **borrowed network**. This type of network is built through someone else's connections, not your own. Instead of forming relationships directly, you're introduced to people through a mutual contact. In other words, someone has to vouch for you and help make the connection. Borrowed networks can be a powerful way to grow your personal or professional circle, especially when you're entering new spaces or industries.

Minorities, women, and young adults face significant challenges when working to establish credibility in environments and industries that are traditionally white-male-dominant and those that associate age with experience. As a result, the network of a mentor or sponsor that has power and influence will help to overcome those challenges, particularly in environments where people of color are underrepresented. In these instances, a borrowed network is paramount to your future success.

Personal Financial Board of Directors

Financial institutions and strong companies have a Board of Directors responsible for formulating goals and strategies for which the institution is to operate. The Board provides clear objectives and a framework in which the company is to achieve its financial goals. The Board ensures that the company is compliant with both internal and external laws, policies, and statutes.

A Personal Financial Board of Directors (PFBOD) is a sounding board that will advise you and provide feedback on your life decisions, opportunities, and challenges. Though your PFBOD doesn't meet or may not be formally identified as a board, they provide unfiltered feedback and true opinions regarding your choices, regardless of how you feel about them. This means you should pick transparent people who will provide an honest perspective regarding your financial goals without being dream busters.

The members of your PFBOD must be diverse and should not include any family members or close friends. Anyone who will provide feedback for the purpose of making you feel good about yourself should not be a member of your PFBOD. Determine the appropriate role for each board member and determine if you prefer some form of accountability regarding accomplishing tasks and goals. The advisory board you create needs to know that you appreciate their input and commitment, whether you actually use the information provided or not. Communicate how much you appreciate their insight and how much it has helped you. However, you are the final decision maker and should take complete ownership of your financial future.

PFBOD advice is predicated on each individual board member's level of financial sophistication. Requests for advice should match experience. It sounds like a no-brainer, but you shouldn't ask the CEO of a successful company to provide you with advice on buying a car. This board member is best suited to answer questions pertaining to the challenges of navigating through a downturn in the economy, strategies on how to increase profit margins, how to attract investors, and how to grow your business.

STARTING A BUSINESS

Starting and managing your own business takes more effort, time, and talent than most jobs ever do. Opening your own business may require personal investment, which poses a significant risk. However, if successful, the reward can be substantial.

According to the SBA, less than 50% of small businesses last more than two years. The reason 95% of these businesses fail is due to the business owner's lack of experience and expertise. Owners with prior experience who thoroughly think through their new business have a far greater chance of success.

Prior to starting your own business, find someone within the industry and ask what it takes to be successful. Volunteer at a similar business to gain experience; ideally, mirror a successful leader. Search for any associations, clubs, or networks to join. This network will help you identify the risks within the industry and how to mitigate those risks.

The PFBOD business owners can help answer questions regarding the initial setup of the business by providing their experiences. The PFBOD can refer to ongoing education, work-shops, courses, guides, and networks that will help increase your chances of success. Lists of government contracting opportunities, business matchmaking events, and grant funding are important discussion topics when speaking with your qualified PFBOD.

If you are interested in starting a business, there are a few preliminary questions that will help facilitate a discussion with someone on your Personal Financial Board of Directors:

- What are the most important skills for a small business owner to have?
- What personality traits do you believe successful small business owners share?
- Of the successful business owners in your neighborhood, what business skills make them successful?
- Do you know any companies that have gone out of business, and what do you think went wrong? How difficult is it to start your own business?

CORPORATE SOCIAL NETWORKING

The best opportunities for upward mobility in your company are through social organizations. The first thing you should do when joining a company is research all of the many social organizations within the company. A trusted work community is the most important yet underutilized space that will propel your career. This community will give you exposure to different ideas, positions within the firm, expert advice on how to do excellent work, and help you identify sponsors who will champion your efforts in rooms you don't have access to.

Strong relationships with upper management promote your reputation and provide support. Conversely, inaccurate or unfair feedback from just one potentially adversarial source, without a strong corporate social network, does considerable harm to your reputation, affecting your future opportunities.

Relationships within a corporate community through these organizations that focus on culture, gender, race, and ethnicity for employees with many different heritages work to grow team members professionally through training, career development, and networking opportunities. The various organizations usually have an extensive calendar full of great events that include community service projects, heritage celebrations, and networking events.

At times, it may feel as though you are unable to build relationships with members of upper management. Joining a social organization at your job will reduce hierarchy and increase accessibility. This network will include Officers, Managing Directors, Executive Directors, and other peers in high-level positions. They would be best able to provide insight into the different personalities of those you're looking to network with in your department or possibly make an introduction. Also, because they may sit in different departments, you will gain exposure to other areas within the company. Building these connections can help you transition into new roles in the company if you have those aspirations.

As is the case within all networks, you will need an elevator pitch to share your background and skills. However, don't talk too much about yourself while networking. The goal is to get to know what others are doing in the company to learn from their experiences while identifying those with whom you would like to build a relationship. Make yourself approachable. Show genuine interest when engaging colleagues and actively listen to learn how you may be able to assist.

Trusted relationships at work may expose you to opportunities that are not yet available to other employees. As an example, if the company is looking to grow and create a new line of business, it will need to fill new positions. If the different roles match your skill sets, you might have an opportunity to advance. At a certain level, most jobs are obtained prior to the formal opening of a position.

"He that walketh with wise men shall be wise: but a companion of fools shall be destroyed." – Proverbs 13:20

My high school teachers would often express this proverb using modern vernacular, stating, "Show me your friends and I'll show you your future," or, as my mother would say, "You are who you hang out with." The principle doesn't change as we age. The concept is even more pertinent when it involves wealth creation and financial success.

Financial discussions within any particular group are likely to happen more frequently amongst successful, financially savvy, well-informed, and financially sophisticated individuals. If your family, friends, and associates are not discussing the economy, new opportunities, business, or the current financial markets, you're not associating with those who can have a positive influence on your future financial success.

In accessing the financial wisdom of others, the objective is not to blindly mimic their behaviors entirely, as market conditions, capital investment, political environments, and local and federal policy may have been different. The key is to use their wisdom and experience to create a personal roadmap to success, developing your own unique approach. The environment in which someone acquired a 100-unit apartment building in South Florida may be different from someone looking to acquire an apartment building in Montclair, New Jersey, but the financial principles, approach, and research required to accomplish the acquisition of a multi-family property will be the same. Quite frankly, no two properties are the same, even if acquired in the same city. The sales price, tenants, leases, property maintenance, and seller's interest will all be different, but the foundational wisdom is the same.

Wisdom is gained along the journey. It's just as important to reflect on your failures as it is to celebrate your successes; there are valuable lessons in both. Proverbs 27:12 says, *"A prudent man foreseeth the evil, and hideth himself; but the simple pass on, and are punished."* This verse highlights the importance of using experience and insight to avoid danger. By studying where others have made financial missteps and how they overcame them, you can better prepare yourself to recognize risks and avoid unnecessary setbacks.

"Where no counsel is, the people fall: but in the multitude of counsellors there is safety." – Proverbs 11:14

Wisdom comes when appropriately using the acquired education, knowledge, skills, and quality experiences in an intelligent, perceptive, and mature manner requiring patience and discernment. Surrounding yourself with people who can provide useful experiences provides foresight, allowing you to draw on their experience to predict your own future success. Increase your probability of success by using the experiences of wise counselors.

Commandment VII
Protection

*"For wisdom is a defence, and money is a
defence: but the excellency of knowledge is, that
wisdom giveth life to them that have it."*
– Ecclesiastics 7:12

F INANCIAL WISDOM IS IMPORTANT and can help protect you
from common financial pitfalls that affect your everyday
life. The Bible puts absolutely nothing above wisdom.
However, the Word proclaims that money is a protection tool as
well. After you've protected yourself financially by acquiring
the wisdom needed to make sound financial decisions and built
a strong savings and an emergency fund, you need to safeguard
the assets and savings you have in place through insurance.

INSURANCE

Insurance is a major expense in many family budgets.
However, the importance of adequate insurance coverage can't
be overstated. Regardless of how savvy you are as a business

professional, how skilled you are as an investor, or even how lucky you are in your current financial situation, being uninsured leaves you vulnerable.

Personal Insurance

Certain professions require greater liability insurance as exposure to lawsuits is commonplace in fields where there is malpractice or regulatory violations. Given the increased probability and frequency of possible lawsuits in these fields, allocate more towards insurance protection. Financial advisors, OBGYNs, real estate agents, and consultants are examples of individuals who will need extended coverage regardless of business insurance coverage.

Homeowners' Insurance

Homeowners' insurance helps to protect you, your home, and your personal belongings from a variety of unexpected events. Unless you purchase a home with cash, mortgage companies will not allow you to finance a home without having the appropriate amount of insurance coverage, which may include flood insurance, depending on the location of the property. It's up to the individual homeowner to ask for more than the standard coverage. A home is often a person's most valuable asset, and you don't want to be underinsured.

Auto Insurance

Each state requires a minimum amount of auto insurance to own and operate a vehicle. Failure to do so can result in severe penalties, including monetary fines and jail time. For instance, the minimum car insurance for New Jersey drivers is:

- $15,000 bodily injury per person per accident
- $30,000 bodily injury for all persons per accident
- $5,000 property damage liability
- $15,000/$30,000 uninsured motorist bodily injury
- $5,000 per accident with $500 deductible uninsured/ underinsured motorist property damage

Be proactive. Understand the requirements in your state and buy enough additional coverage just in case your vehicle is in an accident that results in a lawsuit. As a general rule, your total auto liability coverage should equal your total assets.

> *"Keep me, O LORD, from the hands of the*
> *wicked; preserve me from the violent man;*
> *who have purposed to overthrow my goings."*
> *– Psalms 140:4*

Protecting your personal assets is something I learned fairly early. Some years ago, I had just purchased a new SUV that I was really enjoying for the first few days. It was a Saturday night, and I got a call from a friend who said, "A few of us are catching up in the city, you should meet us there." I figured a night out with friends sounded great. At the time, I was living in a multi-family property I owned on a one-way street. It was two houses from the end of the block and did not have an automatic garage door opener. I backed the car out of the garage and left the rear end of the SUV in the street past a parked car in front of the property. The rear end of the SUV was visible to anyone driving up the block, but it did not restrict the flow of traffic. I got out of the vehicle and walked to the garage door to close it.

I noticed a gold Nissan SUV drive past my vehicle and stop at the stop sign.

The Nissan began to drive in reverse in the wrong direction down the one-way street and hit my new parked car. The guy got out of the car and immediately began apologizing. He said that he was headed to a party at a friend's house in the middle of the block, and drove backwards down the one-way street after he drove past his destination. He'd mentioned that he was driving his wife's car and lied about his location. He pulled his vehicle over and parked a few houses down.

I took several pictures of the damage, including the location of all of the vehicles, the homes and anything else I thought was relevant. I then called the police to file a police report. I told the officer that the other driver was going in reverse down the one-way street. The cop responded, "WHAT?" None of this made it into the police report.

Annoyed, I accepted the fact that my night was over and pulled my new vehicle back into the garage. A few weeks later, my car was out of the shop and I was ready to move past the incident. To my surprise, I received a legal notice in the mail and a call from my insurance company. The driver of the Nissan had decided to file a lawsuit.

The plaintiff said he was parked in front of my driveway, and that I'd backed out and hit him, causing severe mental and physical personal damage. The insurance company discussed the matter with his attorney and the law firm dropped the case. Month after month, I received legal notices from different firms regarding the incident, and they were all dropped. Finally, the plaintiff found a young attorney to represent him in the case.

Five years after the accident, we headed to court.

Interestingly enough, the judge presiding over the case believed the plaintiff. It was apparent she neglected to review the evidence. Fortunately, I chose to use a jury to determine the outcome of the case. The plaintiff was asking for a large settlement amount in the closing argument. After deliberation, the jurors returned to their seats and returned a "not guilty" verdict.

It was found that the plaintiff had previously sued someone he was involved in a car accident with and was successful. This was an apparent pattern he'd used to take advantage of the no-fault laws in New Jersey to manipulate the system and receive settlements.

Taking the initiative to record at the scene, take all the important photos, call the police, demand a police report, and be diligent in the details of what transpired prevented this scammer from winning a judgment against me. Take the extra steps to help ensure the outcome is in your favor.

Umbrella Insurance Coverage

Umbrella Coverage is backup insurance that can be used in instances where your primary coverage is inadequate. In the event that your homeowner, auto, or other liability coverages are exhausted, umbrella coverage pays benefits up to the limit of the policy. For example, if you have $1 million in auto insurance coverage and lose a $2 million judgment, your umbrella policy will pick up the additional $1 million. Otherwise, the plaintiffs could go after your personal assets for damages. Typically, these policies are underwritten for $1 million to $5 million and are very affordable.

Long-Term Care Insurance

Long-Term Care Insurance protects you against the extreme costs of in-home or nursing home care for chronic ailments such as dementia, Alzheimer's, stroke, paralysis, multiple sclerosis, or spinal cord injuries. Other medical care plans are very limited in the coverage they provide. In the absence of long-term care insurance, you could be required to pay more than $200 per day in a nursing home. These expenses can have a significant impact on your overall fiscal health, in which case you may qualify for Medicaid.

In addition, you could develop an ailment prior to acquiring long-term care coverage and be ineligible and therefore denied coverage. Consider purchasing long-term care insurance for your parents if you'll be responsible for their long-term care.

Life Insurance

Children and family are a prized possession; therefore, make sure you have the appropriate life insurance coverage and protections so your family can sustain themselves. Life insurance is also an opportunity to transfer wealth to the next generation. Take out a life insurance policy on your parents so that when they transition, you're able to cash in on a $1 million insurance policy. It's important to have several conversations with your parents about this. The wealthy have always secured the opportunity to increase their wealth over the loss of loved ones. As the least discussed opportunity to create generational wealth, don't shy away from this important conversation.

Life Insurance Premium Finance

Life insurance offers numerous benefits to high-net-worth individuals, including the potential for a tax-free death benefit that will help prevent loved ones from bearing a large financial burden. The favorable tax treatment allows the use of life insurance as a vehicle for estate planning and business succession planning.

Large life insurance policies often come with expensive premiums, which can reduce the amount of cash you have available for other investments. Premium financing can help by covering those payments, so you don't have to sell your investments and trigger capital gains taxes just to pay for the insurance. Depending on the level of financial sophistication, strategic borrowing from well-established financial institutions, wealth management, or private banks may align with your financial goals by optimizing cash flow, maximizing tax efficiencies, and successful estate planning.

Life insurance is effective in wealth preservation, wealth accumulation, and the transfer of wealth. Life insurance is also a great tool to help you achieve your financial goals and objectives.

Asset Protection Trusts

Wealthy individuals often protect their assets by placing them in special legal structures called asset protection trusts. Some choose to create these trusts offshore in places like the Cook Islands or Nevis, though these options can be expensive and complex due to international regulations.

Fortunately, several U.S. states—including Delaware, Rhode Island, Nevada, South Dakota, and Alaska—also allow individuals to set up similar trusts without requiring you to live there.

Here's how these trusts work:

You move certain assets—like cash, stocks, or real estate—into the trust. The trust is managed by an independent trustee, and the people you choose (called beneficiaries) can receive distributions from it. One of the main benefits is that these assets are generally protected from creditors.

To make sure your trust qualifies for asset protection, it must meet a few key requirements:

- It must be irrevocable (meaning you can't change it once it's set up).
- The trustee must be based in the state where the trust is created and licensed to operate there.
- Distributions can only be made at the trustee's discretion.
- All trust documents and management must be based in that state.

Large financial institutions are best suited to establish these trusts as they have the experience and legal expertise.

Staying informed about trust and estate laws is essential if you're managing wealth or planning to pass assets to future generations. As of this writing, the Internal Revenue Service requires estates with combined gross assets and prior taxable gifts exceeding $11.18 million to file a federal estate tax return and potentially pay estate taxes. In contrast, estates valued under that threshold—such as an estate worth $11 million—would not be subject to federal estate taxes or required to file a return.

It's also important to understand the difference between estate tax and inheritance tax. Estate tax is applied before the assets are distributed to heirs, while inheritance tax is applied after the assets are received. Currently, inheritance tax is only enforced in Iowa, Kentucky, Maryland, Nebraska, New Jersey, and Pennsylvania.

Building wealth is only part of the equation—you must also take steps to protect it. Think of it as if you were building a home. No bank will let you close on a mortgage without proof of insurance. In the same way, you should plan for asset protection before the asset is even in your hands. The worst mistake is to build the "castle" without a "moat." Protecting your assets with trusts, insurance, or legal safeguards should be just as intentional as earning or acquiring them in the first place.

BUSINESS STRUCTURES

If you are an entrepreneur, it is important to separate your personal assets from those of the business. If you neglect to take the appropriate legal steps to create a separate business entity, such as a corporation, limited liability company, or limited partnership, a simple dispute could cost you everything you own. There are differences in liability between the various business entities that need to be explored.

Sole Proprietorships

Sole proprietorships offer no limit on personal liability, and one mistake could cost you everything, including your home, depending on the state.

General Partnerships

If your business partner has a personal dispute that has nothing to do with you and loses the lawsuit, the plaintiff's attorney could go after your personal assets. I would not advise setting up a general partnership.

Limited Partnerships

Limited Partnerships have limitations in that you are only liable for the amount you've invested or limited to your ownership percentage. Therefore, you cannot be sued for more than you've invested in the business. The worst-case scenario is that your investment will be wiped out. However, lawyers can't go after your personal assets to settle claims against the business. In a limited partnership, you can't take an active role in the business. If you have an active role, you are no longer a limited partner but will be considered a general partner, and your assets are fair game.

Corporations

Corporations provide excellent asset protection for their owners. Except for cases of egregious fraud, or if you do not treat your corporation as a separate entity, your personal assets cannot be taken in the event your business loses a lawsuit.

Limited Liability Company

Limited liability companies also provide asset protection for their owners. The business entity also allows owners to choose whether to file federal income taxes as a corporation or as a partnership.

If a company loses a lawsuit, a judge may give the winning party shares in the business, which could allow them to see the company's financial records. However, even if they're granted an ownership stake, they can't force the company to hand out cash. Instead, they might still be taxed as if they had received a payout—even when no money was actually given. This tax burden can discourage lawsuits aimed at taking ownership and can sometimes lead to a settlement that's more favorable for the company.

THE HOLY SPIRIT AS A PROTECTOR

The Holy Spirit has several roles and acts as a guide, comforter, and protector. As a guide, the Holy Spirit helps us make the right decisions and aligns us with our purpose. As a comforter, the Holy Spirit provides reassurance and relief from stress, fear, and anxiety. The Holy Spirit is also our protector from both physical and spiritual danger.

The anointing of the Holy Spirit allows for God's greatest protection. We gain favor through faithfulness and obedience to God's will. Our personal relationship with God through constant and consistent prayer, reading the Word, and talking to God daily is how we gain protection through the Holy Spirit. The closer your relationship is with God, the more protection you will have from both physical and spiritual attacks. The

Holy Spirit will protect your assets, your business, spouse, children, family, and friends.

Having God's protection does not mean you will not go through seasons of trials or difficult times. You need challenges and adversity to be transformed into the best new version of yourself. There's a difference between God leading you through a wilderness season to grow and going through a struggle without God's covering or guidance. The former is something you are prepared to handle. In the latter, you are without God's protection. Follow the process of making sure you have everything in place to protect your blessings.

Commandment VIII
Contentment

"He that loveth silver shall not be satisfied
with silver; nor he that loveth abundance with
increase: this is also vanity."
– Ecclesiastics 5:10

CONTENTMENT IS A STATE OF PEACE, firm determination, happiness, and satisfaction, no matter the circumstances. The inner peace that comes from fulfilling one's purpose is living a truly blessed life. In order to live a life of contentment, you must first learn to be grateful. It's impossible to be content without gratitude. In focusing on the good things in your life instead of those things that caused disappointment, you will develop a mindset that promotes and fosters contentment along with a healthy and happy energy.

People who lack contentment often have a "when I get *blank,* then I will be happy" mentality. This is a tragic mistake. Take control of your life and know that your happiness is not reliant on the acquisition of worldly possessions. Happiness is based on the conscious decision to be happy. Once you've decided to be happy, engage in activities that you enjoy and interact with people you enjoy. Avoid environments and people void of happiness. The goal is to let nothing get in the way of living a blessed and fulfilled life.

Lusting after material items and obtaining a lot of money will not make you successful or happy. Our society is obsessed with being unhappy about everything from our appearance to our spouse, our children, the home we live in, elected officials, and even our smartphones. A culture full of distractions and excess has resulted in a need to feed our insecurities through constant comparisons and wasteful spending on luxury items, resulting in depression or other mental health issues.

The Benefits of Being Content

Contentment is a form of trust. Trust that God will provide for your needs. In Matthew 6:26, Christ teaches that if God provides for the birds of the air, you can trust that He will also provide for you. Trust in God and where God is going to take you. The blessing is around the corner if only you submit to God's way and His will.

When Christ is speaking to the multitude, a man asks Jesus to have his brother divide his inheritance with him. Christ's response is that he is not a judge or divider of physical or worldly possessions. The inheritance he comes to bring is that of the Father and what God provides.

Jesus then asks that all take heed and beware of covetousness, as life is not about how much you can consume or obtain. Christ makes it clear that he doesn't want you to lust after or worry about these physical possessions. Christ also states that you should not worry about your next meal or your clothing. Jesus says that God takes care of all of your needs the way he takes care of the lilies. If God is able to take care of these things, He will certainly take care of you.

"Charge them that are rich in this world, that they be not high-minded, nor trust in uncertain riches, but in the living God, who giveth us richly all things to enjoy; That they do good, that they be rich in good works, ready to distribute, willing to communicate; Laying up in store for themselves a good foundation against the time to come, that they may lay hold on eternal life." – 1 Timothy 6:17-19

Contentment is also a form of protection. It protects you from feeling inadequate when you put your faith in God instead of things outside of your control. Contentment protects you from feeling abandoned, left behind, or insecure due to comparisons. Contentment acts as a form of protection, because when you're truly content in all aspects of your life, you're less likely to compromise your values or act in ways that displease God just to fit in or gain material things.

"For we wrestle not against flesh and blood, but against principalities, against powers, against the rulers of the darkness of this world, against spiritual wickedness in high places." – Ephesians 6:12

Contentment is the shield that protects you from those in high places who practice spiritual wickedness. As you grow in the *Spirit,* discernment will remove the veil, and you can plainly see the tricks of the rulers of darkness reflected in the actions of the adversary daily. The enemy uses every medium and frequency to inhibit your light. Malevolent entities that govern the material world will use money or material possessions to convince you that this is the only way. Contentment will suppress these desires of the flesh, which are in opposition to the Spirit.

Contentment helps to build resilience. Persevering through life's many challenges builds character and provides the framework by which we gather the information needed to achieve success. In failure, there is a period of reflection. The first step is to accept that you've failed. Taking ownership of the result allows you to move on quickly. After you've accepted the result, you can then work on adjusting your plan for success. Be grateful for the learning experience and where you are in the process. Galvanize yourself and persist forward, knowing that it's all in God's plan.

Understanding Bad Habits

Bad habits—whether learned or projected onto us—often arise as a way to cope with dissatisfaction, leading us to seek comfort in external pleasures like sugary foods, new clothes, or entertainment. We don't spend much energy determining the root cause. To be content, we must not believe that satisfying our desires through material possessions or pleasures of the flesh will make us whole. The next time you feel discontent, resist the temptation to fall into old spending or eating habits. Instead, commit to gaining a better understanding of why you feel this way and identify the cause. Only after understanding and solving for the root cause and eliminating the need to use these old habits as a crutch will you truly begin to transform and experience contentment.

The Comparison Trap

We often compare the worst of what we know about ourselves to the best assumptions we have of others. Stop comparing yourself to other people. Comparing your life to someone else's will always lead to discontentment and possibly envy. The person you are comparing yourself to is struggling with their own issues, and their life is never as perfect as your mind projects it to be, regardless of what they post on Instagram.

Letting Go

To get to your next blessing, God may need to remove people and material things from your life. Some people in your life may not understand how God is elevating you. Therefore, you must let them go. Certain behaviors, lifestyles, or material items may need to be left behind as you ascend. When you are content, whether you are with or without, you can leave the people, irrelevant superficial lifestyle needs, and material items behind. The absence will allow you to transform into the person you will need to become to achieve greater success. It's harder to evolve into the person you need to be if you're more concerned with what people think of you, especially when you're attempting to live up to a persona or image.

The next destination on the road to success may require relocation. Yes, you may need to drop everything and pick up and leave. There may be a place in the country, or even the world, that will best facilitate your growth and help build new relationships with people God put in your life to help you fulfill your purpose.

Jesus warns those who are overly concerned with obtaining abundance through the story of a rich man whose barn was too small to store all his goods, so he tore down the barn to build a bigger one. By the time the new barn was finished and that barn was filled, God called him home. He transitioned out of the physical world, never being able to use or enjoy all of the abundance that he'd stored.

The reason Christ tells you not to care for your clothes and your home is that it is difficult for you to leave those things behind and follow God. Christ implores you not to care about those things and focus on doing God's work hence the verse, *"And again I say unto you, It is easier for a camel to go through the eye of a needle, than for a rich man to enter into the kingdom of God." – Matthew 19:24.* Proverbs 22:2 also explains, *"The rich and poor meet together: The LORD is the maker of them all."* Show God that He can trust you with riches and continue to do God's work. God will test you. Your job is to pass the test.

Contentment is not Complacency

Believing that material wealth is the key to happiness will leave you empty. However, contentment does not mean complacent. I'm not telling you to give up on your dreams, that there should be no desire to improve, or that you shouldn't want to make a lot of money. However, you should be thankful for what you have, who you are, and appreciate how far you've already come. Improving as a person is an ongoing process, and you can't be complacent. Never stop learning, growing, and achieving.

The warning is not a condemnation of all. It is important to be the exception. Intelligence, understanding, compassion, objectivity, and perspective are not determined by class and socioeconomics, despite the world's affinity for the affluent. While there is much that can be learned regarding success and what it takes to acquire and maintain wealth, God humbles us for our own benefit.

The Word instructs that the rich should not loathe the less fortunate or trust in their material possessions. There can be a sense of entitlement and maybe even selfishness that comes from those who've achieved success. Some put more value on how high they've climbed the corporate ladder and excelled in their careers. Some value status and exclusivity over personal character. Be careful not to put all your trust and value in riches, but in the living God who will provide for all of our needs.

"Let your conversation be without covetousness; and be content with such things as ye have: for he hath said, I will never leave thee, nor forsake thee." – Hebrews 13:5

Foolish and Hurtful Lusts

"Perverse disputings of men of corrupt minds, and destitute of the truth, supposing that gain is godliness: from such withdraw thyself. But godliness with contentment is great gain.

For we brought nothing into this world, and it is certain we can carry nothing out. And having food and raiment let us be therewith content. But they that will be rich fall into temptation and a snare, and into many foolish and hurtful lusts, which drown men in destruction and perdition.

For the love of money *is the root of all evil: which while some coveted after, they have erred from the faith, and pierced themselves through with many sorrows." – 1 Timothy 6:5-10*

The environments in which we can obtain wealth vary and may depend on advantages created by federal and state laws, social constructs, socioeconomics, and the political climate. These environments can heavily influence who becomes wealthy and when, who can bend or break rules and ethics, and who goes to jail. The Bible warns against men of corrupt minds who justify the manner in which they've acquired wealth. The remedy for the lust for riches is contentment. This contentment is centered around the desire to foster a personal relationship with God.

Certain environments promote a culture void of honesty, integrity, and sound business practices, where gross negligence, unethical behavior, and even criminal activity are encouraged to make money by any means. The opportunity to make money should never justify actions that harm another business, individual, or the environment through unfair or harmful treatment. Even with extensive regulations and compliance training across industries, businesses and corporations are still often required to pay millions—or even billions—in fines to government agencies, customers, or both due to regulatory violations and illegal practices.

The verse suggests that "they that will be rich fall into temptation" due to maintaining a lifestyle of excess at the expense of others. Therefore, it takes strong moral character to acquire and manage the blessings of wealth. The wrong lifestyle choice has significant consequences, and contentment is a way to guard against what the Bible describes as the "wilds of the devil," given man's inability to control himself. *"Hell and destruction are never full; so the eyes of man are never satisfied." – Proverbs 27:20*

It is important to remain grounded in the Word so you are both mentally and spiritually prepared to reap God's blessings while fending off temptations that will lead you away from God. *"The blessing of the LORD, it maketh rich, and he addeth no sorrow with it." – Proverbs 10:22*

TEMPTATION

"Then was Jesus led up of the Spirit into the wilderness to be tempted of the devil. And when he had fasted forty days and forty nights, he was afterward an hungred. And when the tempter came to him, he said, If thou be the Son of God, command that these stones be made bread. But he answered and said, It is written, Man shall not live by bread alone, but by every word that proceedeth out of the mouth of God.

Then the devil taketh him up into the holy city, and setteth him on a pinnacle of the temple, And saith unto him, If thou be the Son of God, cast thyself down: for it is written, He shall give his angels charge concerning thee: and in their hands they shall bear thee up, lest at any time thou dash thy foot against a stone.

Jesus said unto him, It is written again, Thou shalt not tempt the Lord thy God.

Again, the devil taketh him up into an exceeding high mountain, and showeth him all the kingdoms of the world, and the glory of them; And saith unto him, All these things will I give thee, if thou wilt fall down and worship me. Then saith Jesus unto him, Get the hence, Satan: for it is written, Thou shalt worship the Lord thy God, and him only shalt thou serve. Then the devil leaveth him, and, behold, angels came and ministered unto him." – Matthew 4:1-11

Testing and trials are part of the process of accessing God's blessings. God will prepare you for your blessing by allowing you to go through battles and adversity, as it builds character and is the best teacher. No one is exempt from these tests and trials.

Satan took Christ to the mountains to tempt him. The reason Christ was able to respond "that man shall not live on bread alone" was because he was content with who he is and who God is. There is a level of desperation that comes with discontent. This desperation will have you make decisions that put you in terrible circumstances and situations.

What is unique about the human experience is that those who are content cannot be tricked into a life of servitude. If you are willing to gain at the expense of your soul, you have lost your freedom. Certain systems are designed to control behavior by keeping us within a limited set of rules. These systems rely on our active participation, often maintained through distractions. Our desires and impulses are exploited for profit, with algorithms tracking how we respond to various stimuli in order to influence our choices.

PREPARING FOR YOUR HARVEST SEASON

God uses a formula to prepare us for our blessings. To make sure you are completely prepared for your blessing, God has created a challenging process specific to you through various trials and tests to make sure you are equipped to handle the blessing. You need to prove to God that the material blessings won't pull you farther away from Him. You will need to show trust in God, and He will need to trust you to complete the task all the way to the end. God knows what it takes for you to be successful at the next level. This transformation process is done through seasons to prepare you for abundance:

(1) a Season of Trials and Tribulations;

(2) a Season of Patience;

(3) a Season of Humility;

(4) a Season of Transformation;

Season of Trials and Tribulations

The season of trials and tribulations, though difficult while in the wilderness, is an actual gift that may only be realized after making it through to the other side. At some point, God will allow you to fail and be weakened. After Jesus fasted for forty days and forty nights and was hungry, therefore weak, the enemy came to tempt him.

Financial difficulty, whether the result of inflation, bank failures, lack of available credit, recessions, currency crisis, or job loss, affects everyone, no matter their socioeconomic status. Financial trials are to be expected, and it's better to be prepared as best you can. To overcome these financial difficulties, it is important to lean heavily on God. He may be trying to get your attention. Read your Bible, especially the Book of Proverbs. Ask God to show you what He wants you to do next. This is a great time to lean on your Personal Financial Board of Directors for guidance. They can help you identify opportunities, develop a strategic plan to get back on track, share their own experiences with similar challenges, offer insights on government efforts to grow the economy, and provide valuable mental and emotional support. Learn to transform a temporary financial setback into God's overflow.

Season of Patience

How you handle trying times will determine how successful you will become. Patience is an important fundamental principle in achieving long-term financial success. A hasty, desperate, emotional financial decision during a difficult time may further exacerbate and complicate an already tenuous situation.

Take time to gather all the information you need to make the right financial decision. There may be an immediate opportunity to correct and pull yourself out of the current financial situation, but don't stress if there isn't an instant solution to your financial setback. Focus on the steps needed to improve one day at a time.

The time it takes to get to your new destination may depend on the severity of the setback. I compare it to my experience with physical therapy. I've gone through physical therapy treatment for various sports injuries, and the rehabilitation was very long and painful. I found that when I completed the full program, I felt great. However, there were times when I did not complete physical therapy for an injury and thought I could skip it. It never turned out well. I either ended up back in physical therapy or needed an additional surgery due to reinjury. I should never have skipped the process. It only resulted in delays and kept me from my goal.

When it comes to financial rehabilitation, do not cut corners or skip steps. If you have patience, you will keep the lessons you learn through this process for a lifetime.

Season of Humility

Humility is an important part of God's process because it makes you strong enough to overcome the need for external validation and prepares you for the increased scrutiny that comes with success. People are going to be very critical of you. You need to be able to objectively and respectfully respond to your family, friends, competitors, and the community, regardless of any unfair agenda. Be careful in how you respond to those who are critical of you. High mental and moral character is an important part of your individual brand.

Humility allows you to think about how you should treat people. People in leadership and with money are watched closely. Negative perceptions pertaining to your interactions with people could close future doors and business opportunities, as people judge you before they ever meet you based on your reputation. Lies travel farther and faster than the truth, so protect your brand and behave accordingly. Don't take the bait. Humility will help you succeed as the Bible provides instruction on how we should treat one another.

I remember thinking I had it all figured out until God humbled me. No matter how hard I tried to get ahead by myself, God would not allow me to succeed. God wanted to make sure He had my full attention. I was busy trying to come up with multiple ways to resolve my financial issues instead of following God's instructions. God was telling me what I needed to do. Instead of trusting Him, I was in a panic trying to figure it out myself.

Remember, even if I follow the instructions up to a particular point, but not all of God's instructions, I would not be allowed to move forward and achieve success. To get through my financial wilderness, I needed to be humbled. It was the only way God could transform me into the person I need to be on the other side. Sometimes you need to be still and wait on the Lord. *"Humble yourselves therefore under the mighty hand of God, that he may exalt you in due time: Casting all your care upon him; for he careth for you." – 1 Peter 5:6-7*

A great way to express contentment through gratefulness and humbleness to God is to share your natural talents and abilities. Helping others will provide perspective and an appreciation for who you are and what you have. The individuals you help will be grateful for the time and resources you contribute to their development and overall well-being. In serving others, you will find that the act is more beneficial to you than to the recipients.

To whom much is given, much is required. Your responsibility will increase as your influence grows, requiring you to set a good example for people who may look up to you. When you've reached a level of success, it's important to recognize the responsibility and influence that comes with it. God wants to ensure you're spiritually prepared for that responsibility and that you understand you were intentionally crafted by Him to help lead others to Him. Since God has exalted you, be sure that you dutifully represent Him in everything that you do. This requires humility.

Season of Transformation

While attending the greatest high school on the planet, I noticed some students were more gifted than others when it came to retaining information and understanding the subject material.

Do I believe all of the guys who got great grades worked harder than others? Absolutely not! There were some students who were just more gifted.

What I did pay close attention to were those students who struggled. I found that those students who were resilient and made ongoing adjustments, accepted that they needed to outwork others to be successful, found support and help, and kept a positive attitude, eventually were able to put it all together and achieve their goals. The fact that they transformed into who they needed to become in order to be successful is what mattered.

Those with an abundance of resources have a competitive advantage. However, it takes more than just resources to be successful. Those who understand how to improve themselves through effort and hard work—and who consistently put in that effort to reach their goals—have developed a vital and valuable skill. I'm confident that when those students who struggled went to college or even faced a particular challenge later in life, they were confident in their ability to develop a plan, streamline their efforts, and find the right people to help them succeed. Our Head Master would tell us to find a sport or extracurricular activity, throw out the television, and focus on where we should be and what we should be doing.

Many self-made millionaires lost all of their money at some point for a variety of reasons. They were able to become millionaires again because of the skills, habits, discipline, and consistency that made them successful in the first place. The wisdom that made them successful, the kind spoken of in the Bible, brought them back to where they needed to be. The lessons learned as a result of financial setbacks are just as invaluable and will help transform you into the best version of yourself.

You need to be very careful when God is transforming you, as the work and development will also make you vulnerable. At that moment, the tempter will approach with a proposition offering you the kingdoms of the world and the glory thereof if you would only fall down and worship the enemy. The enemy knows what blessings God has waiting for you. Stay focused and disciplined. Do not sign the contract. Remember, the Bible doesn't deny that the enemy has the power to fulfill his promises or give you things in this world. However, the cost is too great.

"The blessing of the LORD, it maketh rich, and he addeth no sorrow with it." – Proverbs 10:22

Commandment IX
Prosperity

"A feast is made for laughter, and wine
maketh merry: but money answereth all things."
– Ecclesiastics 10:19

MOST PEOPLE HAVE NEVER READ or made mention of a Bible verse that states that money is the answer to all things. Many of us make the mistake of saying money isn't everything. The Bible says the exact opposite in this verse. In order to build infrastructure, cities, companies, transportation, schools, create jobs, produce food, solve environmental issues, and real-world problems, you need money. The Seventh Commandment (Protection) describes how money is a defense. Here, we see that money is also an answer or a way to solve problems.

If you want to find the root cause of an issue or understand why a particular event transpired, follow the money. When you follow the money, you gain insight into the why. Money answers all, so finding out the monetary motivations behind an event will give you a complete perspective. Furthermore, achieving a positive outcome—whether it's solving a problem or creating something of value—requires money.

Rarely would someone whose medical doctors had instructed them to eat healthy and exercise respond by saying diet and exercise aren't everything. After all, it's not as if the doctor's instructions inherently exclude the importance of other aspects of life, like a relationship with God, family, education, career, and finances. Yet, when it comes to the importance of money as a tool or resource, I've often heard people say that money isn't everything. While the Bible warns us about the lust of money as a road to perdition, the Word also teaches that money is a powerful tool. In reality, solving most problems—whether personal, social, or systemic—requires financial resources. Some solutions come through government funding and incentives, while others are driven by the free market. That's why those with financial means often hold the greatest influence over society; they have the tools to shape outcomes. If you want to influence outcomes in your personal, professional, political, or social life, you'll need access to money in a capitalist society. Otherwise, you'll have to rely on those who have it.

Wealth is rarely built on a single income stream. Instead, it's created by developing multiple sources of revenue, offering value to others, and increasing your earnings through personal expertise. A wise person understands how to earn money, save it strategically, and invest it wisely to generate more income over time.

But proceed with caution. Promises of high returns from risky or impractical ventures often attract those seeking shortcuts. A lazy person will trade discipline for the illusion of easy riches, which usually ends in a significant loss. Diligence, not luck, builds lasting wealth.

You must set the financial foundation before you invest. You need an emergency fund, retirement savings, and a separate savings account dedicated to funding investments, dreams, or future ventures. The *Ten Coin Commandments Biblical Financial System* is designed to prepare you for this moment after you've learned to earn consistently, manage credit wisely, and protect what you've built.

Money without purpose is money you will lose. Savings should be intentional. Idle funds with no clear purpose increase opportunity cost through misuse. But savings with a purpose—earmarked for strategic investments—can become the seed for something much greater.

Start with income. Then save. Then invest. From there, focus on growing your income by adding new revenue streams and maximizing what you already earn. Stay consistent in saving a portion of every dollar you make, and build a strong network. The more connected you are, the more access you'll have to smart opportunities. And when you're prepared, those opportunities turn into wealth.

George S. Clason's book *The Richest Man in Babylon* states, "Gold in a purse is gratifying to own and satisfieth a miserly soul, but earns nothing. The gold we maintain from our earnings is but the start. The earnings it will make shall build our fortunes."

STRATEGIES FOR WEALTH CREATION

While some individuals inherit wealth or happen to encounter a rare life-changing opportunity that skyrockets into a successful generational wealth event, most people who build substantial wealth do so by owning all or part of a thriving business.

A notable group known as HENRYs, High Earners, Not Rich Yet, typically earn between $250,000 and $500,000 annually. Despite impressive incomes, many HENRYs don't accumulate significant wealth due to high taxes, education costs, housing costs, and lifestyle expenses. This underscores an important truth: wealth isn't about how much you make—it's about how much you keep and grow.

Those who break through into true wealth (tens of millions) often follow a similar path. They're entrepreneurs or equity holders, concentrating their time, talent, and money into building a single business. This focused strategy is inherently risky, but when it succeeds, the payoff can be exponential. Their deep involvement in the business gives them both confidence and control, making them more willing to take that risk.

Wealth creation at this level often requires more than just income; it requires ownership, discipline, and strategy.

Below are some of the most common methods used to build and preserve wealth.

Information Publishing

An inexpensive way to earn your financial independence is to create an information publishing company where you provide expert advice, sell ideas, and provide guidance. The information can be sold through various mediums such as e-books, blogs, newsletters, membership websites, podcasts, and seminars.

Information publishing is a great wealth creation strategy because the internet allows for the lowest production costs compared to any other industry. It's possible to sell 100,000 e-books for the same price it takes to produce and sell one physical copy. Take advantage of the new knowledge economy by providing your expert advice on an inexpensive and easy-to-use platform where you can reach your target market and make money by selling valuable information.

Real Estate

Wealth creation through real estate investing is still one of the most popular and lucrative ways to become financially independent. There are several ways to invest in real estate; however, multifamily, mixed-use, or commercial income-producing properties have derived the highest and most consistent returns. Determine the type of real estate investing you plan to participate in and focus on building relationships with individuals who are actively investing in these property types. Create a Board of Directors to provide adequate advice on your real estate investments. Attempting to invest in a broad range of real estate property types where you have very little knowledge or expertise is a recipe for disaster.

Single-family homes, 1-4 family properties, and apartment buildings are all viewed differently and require analysis specific to each property type. Each property type has a different set of risks and significantly different financing requirements. Understand all aspects of these types of real estate investments in order to make an educated decision on where you are comfortable investing.

Focus on real estate assets that are income-producing. If the real estate does not produce income, then think of it as a liability or expense. Don't waste a ton of money or time during your best income-producing years acquiring lifestyle assets (liabilities), which include your primary home. Using your salary to pay for these items is a waste of money. Use the money earned from your various businesses and investments to purchase these items debt-free once you've gotten to that point in your life.

Income-producing real estate is a great hedge against inflation as it provides income, is very well suited for a generational wealth transfer due to favorable US tax laws, has high demand since people need somewhere to live, is resilient and able to withstand political and economic turmoil, and can be leveraged to acquire additional real estate or other income-producing assets.

Business Ownership

Starting a company or having some ownership interest in an entity within an industry that has low-to-medium barriers to entry offers the best upside and flexibility. Partnerships, even at 10% ownership interest, might be the way to go when looking for income-producing opportunities. The commitment to start and run a company by yourself will require your undivided attention. However, if there are a number of competent partners who are capable of creating a solid business plan and have the financial expertise to be successful, a partnership may be the best opportunity to become successful. Be careful in picking your partners. Business is like a marriage where you need to know your partner thoroughly before you decide to commit to starting or investing in a business. Also, depending on your interests and availability, it might be better for you to take a passive investor role where you provide capital but aren't actively involved in the day-to-day operations of the business. Being a passive investor may mean investing in someone else's company. Passive investors don't necessarily influence the success of the companies they are invested in, but let the money do the work.

Stock Investments

Stock market investments are a form of company ownership. When you buy shares of different companies, you gain a partial ownership stake. This can generate a return in two ways: through dividend payments—regular cash payouts some companies give to shareholders—or by selling your shares later at a higher price if the stock value increases.

Investing in company stock can help protect your money from inflation. That's because many businesses are able to raise prices when costs go up, which helps them maintain profits— and potentially grow the value of their stock. Some also pay dividends, which are regular payments made to shareholders, offering a source of income on top of any gains in stock value.

For example, I once worked with a portfolio that brought in over $500,000 a year just from stock-based dividend income.

Of course, not every stock is a smart long-term investment. But if you build and manage a diverse mix of strong, reliable stocks, it can become a powerful tool to grow and pass down wealth from one generation to the next.

In addition to the traditional 401(k) retirement fund provided by your employer or Vanguard (an investment advisory company), look to invest in companies with which you have familiarity and confidence. Do a thorough review of a company's financial reports. Get to know the company by reviewing their financial performance and research management to understand why they are making certain decisions. What is the "street" saying about the direction of the company? Is the company meeting financial projections? What does the earnings report say? Is there reputational risk? Has the company been in the news? Multiple factors influence a company's stock price, and it's important to understand these influences before you invest your hard-earned money.

Commodities

Commodities, particularly gold and other precious metals, have been used as currency and stored by the wealthy for over 2,000 years. Gold and silver are still an integrated part of many cultures around the world as a form of money and a way to preserve wealth over time. While national currencies are no longer backed by gold or silver and there's no official link between precious metals and paper money, gold and silver are still widely seen as a form of real money. Many people trust their value regardless of how their government defines or supports its currency.

Commodities such as gold, silver, aluminum, oil, gasoline, cocoa, steel, and livestock have historically been strong investments because they are durable, easy to trade (liquid), can be divided into smaller units, and tend to increase in value over time. Regardless of whether gold or silver are actually used as money in day-to-day transactions for goods and services, they have the best characteristics for preserving wealth and retaining purchasing power.

While it is best not to blindly follow what other people do, no matter how wealthy they are, it should be noted that many wealthy families own gold. Regardless of the current public opinion of gold and silver, many Swiss vaults are lined with gold bullion from wealthy families who value gold as a permanent storage of wealth.

Collectibles

A collectible is an item that either currently has value (wealth preservation) or will have greater future value (speculation) as a collectible item. Examples of collectibles are paintings, artwork, stamps, vintage wines, coins, rugs, or cars. The different types of items people collect may be limitless. However, most collectibles acquired by wealthy families are already considered valuable, eliminating speculation regarding the future value, as the value is likely to increase over time. Wealthy families already have a significant amount of wealth. Therefore, the goal is not only to grow wealth, but to preserve it. Preservation is the priority. This is more important than any speculation regarding future value.

Collectibles are a favored asset class. The items are typically purchased for some personal enjoyment, but also accomplish the goal of being a hedge against inflation. There aren't many investments where one gets personal enjoyment and asset value appreciation at the same time.

SUCCESSION PLANNING

It's a mistake to believe that wealth created and acquired in one generation will continue to grow in subsequent generations.

Without proper planning, the wealth could easily be lost in future generations due to taxes, high professional service fees, poor investments, and unprepared recipients' excessive spending.

It is important to create a roadmap that outlines the direction for future financial sustainability. The financial plan should clearly reflect how the wealth should be managed and invested for future generations. The financial plan should also incorporate tax planning strategies to minimize the effect of taxes. Employ a financial planning professional who specializes in your area of focus, as well as one who has experience advising clients with a similar asset size, who can incorporate the appropriate strategies.

Investment in Financial Education

Education is extremely important if the family wants their wealth to last multiple generations. While higher education in the form of college and graduate degrees is important, it is more important to have education in the form of experience and wisdom passed down from those family members who have either earned wealth or have experience managing it successfully.

Wealthy families are able to build wealth and sustain it for multiple generations through the education of family members. Nelson Rockefeller told of how his father gave each of his children an allowance of 25 cents, but if they wanted more money, they had to earn it by working. He also required that they account for where all their money went. These types of lessons are important to pass down to the next generation.

While it is important for every family to teach children about money and wealth, the burden of large amounts of wealth can be difficult for inexperienced family members to manage on their own. There are many examples of professional athletes, lottery winners, and winners of substantial legal settlements receiving large sums of money with little experience and subsequently losing it due to a lack of experience in managing it.

Seek finance professionals to teach your children. The financial world evolves very quickly, and you want to ensure you have the most up-to-date information. Financial advisors, attorneys, and tax professionals are an important part of this process. Each should be sought out for skills that match the family's needs. How money is made, invested and preserved has evolved, given significant technological advancements. Having an expert guide the next generation into the future of wealth management is imperative.

Prosperity & Wealth Preservation

Strategies for preserving wealth are different from those used to generate it. Rather than putting all your money in one place, spread your investments across stable, low-risk markets. Diversification helps protect you from major losses. You can also reduce your overall risk by avoiding too much borrowing (leverage) and building in a financial cushion or margin of safety.

You don't need to take huge risks to grow your wealth. Over the past decade, a globally diversified portfolio made up of 70% stocks and 30% bonds more than doubled in value. While this strategy may not yield overnight riches, it offers steady, reliable growth that can build significant wealth over time.

Importantly, focusing on preserving wealth doesn't mean sacrificing strong returns. A balanced, long-term investment approach can still produce impressive results, especially when compounded over time.

Even after a successful business is sold, it's important to place the proceeds into a safe investment vehicle that will generate consistent income. Do not take those proceeds and throw them into a new business as the immediate next step. Future success is not predicated on prior achievements, and there is no guarantee that you'll catch lightning in a bottle the second time. Allocate at least 80% of the proceeds into investments that are reliable and will preserve your wealth over time. The remaining 20% will be invested in new ventures, which may yield great returns but also may be completely lost if you choose the wrong investment strategy.

If you're self-employed or own a small business, you're probably hurting your own financial future if you haven't opened a Simplified Employee Pension (SEP) or Individual Retirement Account (IRA) plan. These are relatively easy and inexpensive to administer. An individual or solo 401(k) can also provide a good combination of benefits to a self-employed person.

Professional services from business consultants, financial advisors, wealth management professionals, and accountants are an important part of your financial team and will provide the necessary guidance. They are worth every penny. The cost of poor financial decisions and missed opportunities takes years to recover from and adds significant stress.

THINK, STUDY, DO

"This book of the law shall not depart out of thy mouth; but thou shalt meditate therein day and night, that thou mayest observe to do according to all that is written therein: for then thou shalt make thy way prosperous, and then thou shalt have good success." – Joshua 1:8

"The book of the law (Holy Bible) shall not depart out of thy mouth" is telling the reader that the Word is not for regurgitation if you are looking for success. The instruction is to meditate (think deeply and carefully) therein day and night that one may observe (study) and **DO** according to **ALL** that is written therein. Though we get caught up in spirited debates on what the Bible says, the revelation of God requires us to actually live the Word.

Only after studying and doing all that is written in the Bible will you then have a roadmap to success and become prosperous. Making thy way prosperous means you have to actively do something to create a pathway for yourself. The Bible equips you with the necessary tools to be successful. This is not a magic carpet ride. The entire process requires you to actively participate. Again, the verse doesn't say, and then you will walk in prosperity. In order to make your way through something, you will be challenged, and there will be adversity. If you're prepared for the challenges, you will have the confidence and faith to overcome them.

TREE OF LIFE

"Now about that time Herod the king stretched forth his hands to vex certain of the church. And he killed James the brother of

John with the sword. And because he saw it pleased the Jews, he proceeded further to take Peter also. (Then were the days of unleavened bread.) And when he had apprehended him, he put him in prison, and delivered him to four quaternions of soldiers to keep him; intending after Easter to bring him forth to the people. Peter therefore was kept in prison: but prayer was made without ceasing of the church unto God for him. And when Herod would have brought him forth, the same night Peter was sleeping between two soldiers, bound with two chains: and the keepers before the door kept the prison. And, behold, the angel of the Lord came upon him, and a light shined in the prison: and he smote Peter on the side, and raised him up, saying, Arise up quickly. And his chains fell off from his hands. And the angel said unto him, Gird thyself, and bind on thy sandals. And so he did. And he saith unto him, Cast thy garment about thee, and follow me. And he went out, and followed him; and wist not that it was true which was done by the angel; but thought he saw a vision. When they were past the first and the second ward, they came unto the iron gate that leadeth unto the city; which opened to them of his own accord: and they went out, and passed on through one street; and forthwith the angel departed from him. And when Peter was come to himself, he said, Now I know of a surety, that the Lord hath sent his angel, and hath delivered me out of the hand of Herod, and from all the expectation of the people of the Jews. And when he had considered the thing, he came to the house of Mary the mother of John, whose surname was Mark; where many were gathered together praying. And as Peter knocked at the door of the gate, a damsel came to hearken, named Rhoda. And when she knew Peter's voice, she opened not the gate for gladness, but ran in, and told how Peter stood before the gate. And they said unto her, Thou art mad. But she constantly affirmed that it was even so. Then said they,

It is his angel. But Peter continued knocking: and when they had opened the door, and saw him, they were astonished. But he, beckoning unto them with the hand to hold their peace, declared unto them how the Lord had brought him out of the prison. And he said, Go show these things unto James, and to the brethren. And he departed, and went into another place."
– Acts 12:1-17

The road to prosperity is outlined here in Acts. The revelation provides a level of detail within the passage that, if understood and followed meticulously, will lead to sustained prosperity. The story also describes the many difficulties on the road to prosperity. Let's review the steps to prosperity outlined in the passage.

Step 1: Prayer

Herod placed Peter in prison with four soldiers to keep him captive to prevent his escape. However, prayer was made without ceasing unto God for him. The first step toward a prosperous life is having a group of prayer warriors who pray for one another's success, asking God to remove all obstacles and to direct your paths.

Prayer is to be done without ceasing. Spend time in prayer and speak to God multiple times each day individually. Utilize prayer with your group at least once a week. When there are serious events, you need to pray as a group immediately and every single day until you achieve the desired result. The power of prayer is real. Since new blessings bring new devils, you have to be spiritually grounded to deal with the devil at the next level. Do not pray that God take you to the next level if you're not willing to fight the adversary waiting for you when you get there.

"Put on the whole armour of God, that ye may be able to stand against the wiles of the devil. For we wrestle not against flesh and blood, but against principalities, against powers, against the rulers of the darkness of this world, against spiritual wickedness in high places." – Ephesians 6:11-12

Step 2: Obey God's Instruction

Herod was to have Peter executed in the morning. Peter was sleeping between two soldiers and bound by two chains in his prison cell. In addition, Herod had two soldiers outside the door of Peter's cell. The enemy had the material resources, an army, and political support to execute Peter.

God sent an angel to Peter's cell who tapped him on the side, began to raise him up, and told him to get up quickly. Upon hearing the instruction, Peter got up and the chains fell off. Peter didn't complain to God about his circumstances or condition.

If you've ever tried to physically lift someone up, you know it's extremely difficult to do so if that person doesn't participate. An unconscious person who feels like dead weight is hard to move. Therefore, Peter needed to actively get up as the angel assisted him.

No one can save you from your current financial situation if you do not participate in your own liberation. God told you to start a business, apply for a new job, ask for a promotion, buy apartment buildings, or start a retail clothing business. God said, Get up. God then put people in your life to assist you in making your dream a reality. God didn't ask you how you felt about it. God didn't ask you whether or not you thought it was possible. God sent an angel who instructed you to get up. After you follow the instruction, God then removes all that stands in your way.

God already knew what Peter was going through and what he needed. When God sends you someone who then says, Get up, don't complain or make excuses about your situation or circumstance. If God can deliver Peter, He can deliver you from your current condition.

Your doubt is the reason you feel God hasn't moved in your life and the reason you feel incapacitated. The truth is, God told you to get up, and instead of following his instruction, you decided to complain and make excuses. Realize that you will not get to your blessing unless you follow God's instruction. If Peter complained and made excuses about the soldiers on each side of him, the two soldiers outside the prison door, or the chains restricting him, he would have been executed. However, instead of talking about what appeared to be impossible, he followed the angel's instructions and got up.

The angel then gave Peter further instruction by telling him to put on his sandals. The Bible says that Peter then followed the instruction, "And so he did." The angel then told Peter to put on his clothes and follow him. Peter did as instructed. Peter put on his clothes and followed the angel.

Be sure to follow ALL of the instructions. God will not allow you to move forward without first following the instruction he has already given. If Peter had not gotten up, he would have never received the next set of instructions. Do not look ahead.

Follow the instruction before moving on. If you do not follow the instruction, you will not be given the next set of instructions and you will remain where you are. Let me be the first to tell you, God will make you wait days, weeks, months, years, or the rest of your life. It's really up to you. Go back and follow the instruction so you can move forward and receive your blessing. Your submission and cooperation are important to your success. Trust God.

Sometimes you will not be instructed to lead, but to follow. The best leaders were first great followers. If you are instructed to follow, please accept your role and do so. We can exhibit leadership while following. However, if God is taking you somewhere, allow him to use another person to take you where you could not take yourself. The time will come when the person leading you can't take you any further. God will then give you another set of instructions, which may be to lead.

Step 3: The Vision

God will reveal Himself and your set of instructions by using the Holy Spirit and angels to communicate through a vision. Sometimes, you will experience this vision through seeing a recurring number within a period of time. If you see the same number on multiple occasions, write the number down and research its meaning. In other instances, God will reveal what's to come through dreams, recurring feelings, or a sense that you were here before and that you are exactly where you are supposed to be.

In Acts, Peter didn't believe that what he was experiencing was real, but that he saw a vision. When God is elevating you, it often feels like a dream and it is too good to be true. Just keep going. Your prayers and faithfulness, through actively following the instructions, are fulfilling, and the accomplishments will be more than you could have ever imagined. Ask God to reveal what he wants you to do and where you need to go.

Upon receiving a vision, it's ok to ask God for confirmation, similar to Gideon in the Book of Judges. Gideon asked God for confirmation by putting a fleece of wool on the ground and asked that in the morning the earth be dry and the fleece be full of dew. God did so, and the next morning the fleece was full of dew and the ground was dry. Gideon asked God for further confirmation, asking that the next morning the ground be full of dew and the fleece of wool be dry. God did so, and the next morning the ground was full of dew and the fleece of wool was dry. At that moment, Gideon knew that it was God and that what God promised would come true. Ask God to confirm his promise in your own way. God will make himself known and confirm what's been revealed to you.

Step 4: Walk Through the Door

Peter followed the angel past the first and second ward and came to the iron gate that led to the city. The iron gate opened to them on its own accord without being touched or commanded to do so. When something is done on its own accord, it is done automatically.

When God opens a door, all you need to do is walk through it. The hard work to get to this point is paying off, and the only thing you need to do is take full advantage of the opportunity. God will remove you from a bad situation and place you in a new space at a different level with a new opportunity. It will be obvious that this new opportunity is the work of God by the way everything aligns perfectly. Prepare for your blessing by putting in the necessary work to set yourself up for success, and be ready to walk through the door.

After exiting the gate, Peter and the angel walked past one street. Peter then realized that it wasn't a dream, and the angel departed. The time for Peter to follow had passed, and now Peter was on his own.

In life, there are times when God will hold your hand the entire way. There are also times when God has taken you as far as He's going to, and the rest is up to you. Sometimes, we hang onto people too long that we need to cut loose so we can transition into the next phase of our life. Realize that walking through the door may also require you to let go. Moving on isn't always easy, but know that in order for you to move forward, you may need to leave some people or things behind.

I remember asking God for a promotion at my job. God replied that I could not get a promotion because I was wasting money on sneakers that I didn't even wear. God told me that I couldn't want the respect of men and be productive in a new position, dressing like a child. God told me I needed to dress for my next role, and prepare and think as if I were already in the position. I needed to make these changes in order to transform into someone who would be successful in the role. I made those adjustments immediately and was promoted to a very visible management position at a fairly young age. I needed to leave a mindset, old clothes, and irresponsible spending habits behind in order to walk through the door.

Step 5: Persist

Peter goes to Mary's house, where a few are gathered and praying. Once again, it is the power of people gathered together to pray. Peter knocks on the gate, and a young woman comes to the gate and realizes that it's Peter. Instead of opening the gate, she runs with excitement to tell those in the house. Most of us would instinctively think, Why in the world did the young lady not immediately open the door, considering all that's transpired and the level of danger facing Peter? The best course of action would be to open the gate immediately and let Peter in. The woman, though excited about Peter being free from prison, did not have the authority to open the gate. So, she ran back inside to convince the gatekeepers who had the authority to open the gate.

In life, you will have people who can champion your talent, gifts and abilities. Sometimes you need someone who can put you in front of a gatekeeper to open the next door. This could be someone on your Personal Board of Directors who is willing to leverage their relationships to get you the exposure needed to get you to the next level.

Rhoda was persistent and passionate about what she saw. She did not give up despite the number of times the gatekeepers rejected her and didn't believe what she was saying. While Rhoda was inside telling the gatekeepers that Peter was alive and outside the gate, Peter was also persistent in knocking on the gate.

Gatekeepers want to be sure that you are someone who is going to give it your all. They want to know that no matter how hard it gets, you have the perseverance to keep going. They need to know that you really want what you're looking for and you're not a waste of their time. Perfect your craft, be diligent, and persist.

Step 6: Testify

After Peter was let in, he asked that they hold their peace. Peter then began to profess what God had done. This is an extremely important point in your journey to success. If you are NOT willing to give God the glory for what he has done, why would he bless you again? Some of us fail to even acknowledge that God is the reason we are successful and pretend that we made it here all by ourselves.

Not only are you to provide your personal testimony and glorify God for what He's done, like Peter, but also make sure your actions are so in tune with God that those who interact with you know and profess you must be blessed by God.

Step 7: Exit

When Peter escaped from prison, he went to the home of Mary, the mother of John, where many were gathered and praying. After providing a testimony, he told everyone to spread the word of how the Lord brought him out of bondage. The last thing Peter did was leave.

The financial landscape can evolve so quickly that it is important to be very agile and continue to evolve in this fast-paced digital and global world economy. Market timing involves moving investments in or out of financial markets. Exiting a financial market at the right time allows you to lock in profits and avoid losses from unfavorable conditions or a declining asset. This strategy also helps preserve long-term investments, which is especially important when those assets are intended to provide retirement income. Emotional bias and greed can lead us to want to linger in bad situations despite the obvious signs. If God was able to take you out of a dangerous situation, leave it. The reason to exit should be logical rather than emotional. Managers of financial investments should be able to clearly state the reasons for exiting in the same way they were able to define their reasons for investing.

When determining if you should exit, read economic reports. Metrics on GDP growth, inflation rates, and employment data provide insight into market health. An economy that is slowing can signal the opportunity to exit to preserve gains.

Stock indicators like moving averages, the Relative Strength Index, and stock trading volume can signal when it's a good time to sell. These metrics should also be used to determine buy opportunities in a bull market.

Clearly defined return goals before you enter into an investment or business venture provide a measure for when to exit. Predetermined expectations will prevent you from chasing uncertain gains. Pre-set thresholds, such as stop-loss or take profit levels, remove emotions from the decision. A percentage exit strategy is a straightforward approach where you set predefined thresholds for exiting based on percentage gain or loss. For example, you may decide to sell an asset after a 20% gain or sell the asset after a 10% decline in value to limit losses. Discuss any exit decisions with a trusted advisor, mentor, or financial planner to get their perspective. Cash from a well-executed exit through the sale of a business or the end of an existing partnership can lead to new opportunities and increased personal liquidity.

Worship God For His Blessings

"And thou say in thine heart, My power and the might of mine hand hath gotten me this wealth. But thou shalt remember the LORD thy God: for it is he that giveth thee power to get wealth, that he may establish his covenant which he sware unto thy fathers, as it is this day. And it shall be, if thou do at all forget the LORD thy God, and walk after other gods, and serve them, and worship them, I testify against you this day that ye shall surely perish. As the nations which the LORD destroyeth before your face, so shall ye perish; because ye would not be obedient unto the voice of the LORD your God."
– Deuteronomy 8:17-20

Some of us successful folk forget where we came from and who got us there. We sit in church and don't want to praise God for how far He's brought us. We sit in the pew staring at those who would be perceived as less fortunate, wondering why they shout and are so undignified. When the preacher gives the instruction to speak to your neighbor, you remain fixed or provide an "I-am-above-this" disposition, smirk at your fellow worshipper and immediately return your eyes forward.

The officer title at our current place of employment or business has made us believe that our success is the result of our own abilities and not God's grace. The verse is a reminder that He gave you the power to get wealth and be successful. Therefore, you should be leading the worship parade, given all that God has blessed you with.

Commandment X
Give

"By him therefore let us offer the sacrifice of praise to God continually, that is, the fruit of our lips giving thanks to his name. But to do good and to communicate forget not: for with such sacrifices God is well pleased." – Hebrews 13:15-16

GOD INSTRUCTS US to give through praise. Christ came to sanctify the people with his own blood through his suffering. In Christ, we may now be forgiven for our sins. However, we are still required to make a sacrifice. That sacrifice is the gift of praise unto God, giving thanks to Christ. The sacrifice of praise is to be given continually. The first thing you should do when you wake up is give God praise. Take time throughout the day to connect with God through praise.

The second instruction is also an important part of the required sacrifice. God explains that the second sacrifice is to do good. The people are to honor Christ's sacrifice by doing good and not evil. To selfishly look to gain by any means is a sin, especially when your actions have a disparate impact. A disparate impact is when policies or practices appear to be neutral on the surface, but result in unequal outcomes and sometimes even unintentional disparities. It's not just about the intention but the actual results. The people of God are required to give praise through Christ and do good works, as we are representatives of the divine.

The last sacrifice is to communicate. When the Bible speaks of communication, it does not mean to argue or debate. The purpose of communication is to provide important information, speak kindness, and speak with the purpose of uplifting others, emphasizing encouragement. Biblical communication is to strengthen relationships, improve understanding, and build one another up. The purpose of communication is to show love, truth, respect, salvation, understanding, and harmony. *"Let no corrupt communication proceed out of your mouth, but that which is good to the use of edifying, that it may minister grace unto the hearers." – Ephesians 4:29.*

As individuals, we've learned to communicate differently depending on our environment. However, the Word says that the Spirit of God lives in you! Therefore, we should speak in accordance with the Word, always guided by the biblical purpose of communication.

Give God praise through Christ, do good and not evil, and communicate with the purpose of edification. The Bible speaks of the tongue as having the power of life and death. The Bible calls for us to speak life into one another. This is what pleases God.

While in prayer, thank God for the specific blessings He has provided you. Acknowledging what God has done for you removes anything attempting to get in the way of your financial goals. It is a way of surrendering your heart to God. As a result, God will cover you. God needs to know that He can trust you and that you will not be corrupted.

"Remove far from me vanity and lies: give me neither poverty nor riches; feed me with food convenient for me: Lest I be full, and deny thee, and say, Who is the LORD? or lest I be poor, and steal, and take the name of my God in vain."
– Proverbs 30:8-9

THE IMPORTANCE OF COMMUNITY

"I have coveted no man's silver, or gold, or apparel. Yea, ye yourselves know, that these hands have ministered unto my necessities, and to them that were with me. I have showed you all things, how that so laboring ye ought to support the weak, and to remember the words of the Lord Jesus, how he said, It is more blessed to give than to receive." – Acts 20:33-35

Idolatry is manifested in many ways. You may find that some people worship other individuals for their accomplishments or social status. Some worship money and material resources. Some worship organizations they belong to, while others worship their phones and the attention they receive via likes on social media. This verse is important because it begins with Paul's affirmation that he is clean, sanctified, and pure, having no greed, idolatry of wealth, or lustful motivations. By this confession, in revealing that he has no idols, he gains the trust of those he is serving as a spiritual leader.

Developing strong character is essential on your financial journey. Paul's actions, as observed by others, served as a means to provide not only for his own needs but also for those who depended on him.

In business, contracts are based on mutual benefit between the parties involved. Each person in the transaction receives something of value that reflects their experience, service, skills, or contribution. Everyone working on a project is paid their fair share. Whether compensation comes in the form of money, food, clothing, or shelter, it's distributed fairly among the group.

Traditionally, our compensation is based on our level of experience and productivity, which is fair. The verse takes it a step further. In this verse, Paul insists that by his hands and through his work (laboring), he is only providing support for his necessities, for those with him, and for those who are weak. In honoring the words of Christ, *"It is more blessed to give than to receive."*, God is the provider of every good thing. God, through our obedience, work, and stewardship, is able to provide for all. This does not contradict the Second Commandment, Work, as those who are able-bodied need to be productive members of the community. The weak, who may include the youth, elderly, or less fortunate, are those who need our support.

TITHING

"Will a man rob God? Yet ye have robbed me. But ye say, Wherein have we robbed thee? In tithes and offerings. Ye are cursed with a curse: for ye have robbed me, even this whole nation. Bring ye all the tithes into the storehouse, that there may be meat in mine house, and prove me now herewith,

saith the LORD of hosts, if I will not open you the windows of heaven, and pour you out a blessing, that there shall not be room enough to receive it." – Malachi 3:8-10

The idea of tithing is heavily debated, well…at least amongst parishioners. Many don't believe that tithes and offerings go to God, but instead support the church and pay the pastor's salary. Though this is true, the concept of trusting God by giving back ten percent of what he's blessed you with or by giving your first fruits is real. God asks you to test him, and He will open the windows of heaven and pour out a blessing that there shall not be room enough to receive it.

My Tithe Got Me a Job

God tested me with my tithes, and His Word about pouring out a blessing proved to be true. The recession in 2007 caused banks to make staffing cuts, and I was let go during layoffs. At the time, I was living in a two-family property that I owned, and all I could think about was how long I had before my savings ran out, causing me to no longer be able to pay the mortgage.

One Sunday in church, I heard God say, Bring me $500.00. Now, $500 was significant to me, especially since I no longer had a job. I heard God's voice again say, "Bring me $500.00." I said, "God, I just lost my job and need to pay my mortgage," as if God didn't know that already. God said, "Well, you can save the money and never get a job and lose the house I gave you, or you could trust me and tithe so I can give you a blessing." I said, "Ok God. This $500.00 is for multiple banks to offer me a position, and I get to pick my salary." God said, "DONE."

That Monday, I got calls from at least five banks asking for my services. I hadn't even applied to most of them. When I asked how they got my contact information, the talent manager said he saw my resume online and thought I would be a good fit. I scheduled several interviews and was successful in getting multiple offers. I picked the best job, and stated and received the salary I wanted.

My Tithe Got Me A Promotion

My manager was retiring, and there was an opportunity to manage Business Banking Credit underwriters throughout the Tri-State (NY, NJ, CT) who analyzed complex companies and industries. The position was highly visible and required a significant level of leadership and responsibility. The department had received negative reviews from the bank's internal audit, and the person hired as the Credit Analyst Manager would play an important part in improving the department's audit results. There were portfolio management issues, and the line of business was feeling pressure all the way up to the CEO of the bank.

After meeting with the current manager for advice, I prepared for multiple interviews based on his guidance. I prepared for any type of question that could be asked during the interview process and went through all the work I'd submitted as an underwriter. I felt prepared for the interviews and believed I would be successful in the role. The Sunday before the week of interviews, I gave my tithe, asking God for the promotion to this management position. God told me to go to work after church and pray in the conference room where the interviews would be held. He told me to anoint the rooms so that He would be present with me during the interview. God also told me to pray for favor in the eyes of the interviewers, and I did.

My interview for the position was the best interview I had ever had. I told my future boss and the Senior Credit Officer that I had a plan that would fix all of the issues. In the interview, I provided a presentation of the credit process I would implement that would change the results of our next audit and resolve the department's credit and portfolio management issues within 90 days. I was the youngest person applying for the position and had zero management experience. Still, they were impressed with my interview and my level of preparation. Upper management believed I would deliver the results and gave me the opportunity.

A week hadn't gone by when I walked past a colleague who said, "You know if you don't deliver, you're getting fired, right? There is zero room for error." I looked at him with a grin, nodded my head slowly, and said, "Ok!" I told myself that pressure makes diamonds. I knew I had the perfect plan, but I needed support from my manager to execute.

When I stepped into the new role, I knew I'd face resistance, especially from sales managers set in their ways. But I also knew that if I wanted real change, I'd need full support from leadership. I asked my manager for full autonomy, and thankfully, he backed me. We aligned on a plan, but just 30 days in, the Regional President gave me a tighter deadline; I now had 30 days to deliver results. I didn't panic. I trusted God and got to work. I visited every site, worked long hours, and rallied the teams across multiple states. By the end of the 60 days, we'd transformed the culture, cleaned up the portfolio, and passed the audit with flying colors. The success gained national attention, and that moment reminded me that when you lead with faith and follow through with action, the doors will open.

My Tithe Made My Enemy My Footstool

Success in my new position as the Credit Analyst Manager for the Northeast had me in the clouds for the first few months. However, as I said before, new blessings bring new devils. My year-end review was excellent. I had the best manager, was part of the best leadership team in the bank, and my underwriting team members were very competent and doing an excellent job.

Unfortunately, the New Jersey sales manager wasn't performing well and tried to shift the blame to the credit department. He claimed his team couldn't bring in qualified loan applicants because my underwriting team either didn't support them or rejected good deals. While it's true the bank had strict lending standards—stricter than any I've seen, there were still solid opportunities. The real issue was a lack of credit knowledge on his team, which he expected us to make up for. Instead of addressing that, he singled me out as the reason for the region's poor results—a move I found both unprofessional and unfair. He'd identified a scapegoat. God had other plans.

In the end, God made my enemy my footstool. Despite the sales manager's tactics to save his job by employing various strategies to end mine, his inability to accept responsibility for the low sales numbers and make the appropriate adjustments led to his departure. God's covering over the blessings He promised is always greater.

TIME & EXPERIENCES

Giving isn't always a monetary exercise. The best gifts are shared time and experiences. Spending time pouring into others is a gift that benefits individuals within the community and creates trust.

While volunteering at a fast-food chain to better understand the restaurant industry, I gained insight into its corporate culture, which placed a strong emphasis on community involvement. As a business owner, being present in the community and providing goodwill is important to the ecosystem of the neighborhood. When the community sees that you're not just there to take their money and leave, patrons will go out of their way to support your business because they think of you as an important part of their community. Engaging with the community helps businesses build and strengthen relationships with the local residents and social organizations, which increases exposure and leads to a more loyal customer base.

Community involvement boosts business visibility and fosters a strong reputation as a responsible, caring brand. The goodwill generated through local engagement often extends beyond your immediate market, increasing brand awareness and expanding the company's reach into other communities. Businesses that demonstrate a commitment to the community differentiate themselves from their competitors and gain a competitive advantage.

Businesses that are committed to the community are attractive to potential employees who want to work for a company that cares. A company that cares about the community also cares about its team members. The work environments in these companies poll very well, with higher retention rates than businesses that are not involved.

Businesses create a more vibrant and sustainable community by supporting local initiatives and fostering a sense of belonging. Community involvement leads to improvements in education, healthcare, arts and culture, the environment, and many areas that enhance the quality of life for residents.

Employee Volunteering Opportunities

Every company I've worked for has provided a way to participate in community service. Community involvement provides opportunities to network with others and get exposure to different roles and responsibilities within the company. Building relationships with caring people within your organization creates a sense of belonging. No one is responsible for your career. However, by taking the initiative to build long-lasting relationships with people who care for one another's well-being, you are taking ownership of your career and adding trajectory to your aspirations by building a strong corporate network.

Many community events include a number of different companies and organizations. Networking within the industry is also a great opportunity to learn about what other companies are doing. Building a strong network within the industry gives you greater flexibility and builds your personal and professional brand. This network will give insight into other companies' corporate culture, which may be vastly different than what you'd prefer, or possibly exactly what you're looking for.

"Woe unto you, scribes and Pharisees, hypocrites! for ye pay tithe of mint and anise and cummin, and have omitted the weightier matters of the law, judgment, mercy, and faith: these ought ye to have done, and not to leave the other undone."
– *Matthew 23:23*

LIGHTS IN THE WORLD

"For it is God which worketh in you both to will and to do of his good pleasure. Do all things without murmurings and disputings: That ye may be blameless and harmless, the sons of God, without rebuke, in the midst of a crooked and perverse nation, among whom ye shine as lights in the world; Holding forth the word of life; that I may rejoice in the day of Christ, that I have not run in vain, neither laboured in vain."
– *Philippians 2:13-16*

The work of God is to be done by us who receive him. In the image of God, our works are a light that shines in a perverse nation. Submission to the will of God removes all blame. We must align our finances with Biblical principles through obedience, discipline, and by honoring God with what He's provided.

The 10 Coin Commandments Biblical Financial System is designed to bring you closer to God, through prayer and obedience, to do good work, communicate, and be an example of light in the world. The System helps you rise above the many schemes that would funnel you into confusion and bondage. As previously mentioned, money is a tool. The enemy uses money as a weapon to divide, bring you into bondage, and restrict God's light to control you. My goal is for you to be free. This freedom is spiritual, mental, physical, and financial.

The world is redefining good as evil, and that which is evil is now good. *The 10 Coin Commandments Biblical Financial System* provides clarity, bringing you back to the source of all financial wisdom.

- **Commandment I** is about searching for the Wisdom & Instruction that will make you successful in your financial endeavors.

- **Commandment II** is about productive Work that earns income.

- **Commandment III** helps you develop a sound financial plan.

- **Commandment IV** teaches you the importance of saving to cover unforeseen challenges.

- **Commandment V** discusses potential credit opportunities and the penalties of poor debt management.

- **Commandment VI** employs you to surround yourself with wise counsel who will provide the appropriate perspectives and guidance.

- **Commandment VII** covers various forms of protection as we need God's covering.

- **Commandment VIII** builds character, eliminates jealousy, and allows you to appreciate what God has already done!

- **Commandment IX** teaches you how to handle prosperity, which is very difficult given the barrage of constant stimuli.

- Finally, **Commandment X** is about honoring the sacrifice Christ made for us through our giving.

Closing Prayer

*Heavenly Father, You are the LORD of
breakthroughs. In Your Word, it is promised
that You will open up the windows of heaven
and pour out a blessing that there is not enough
room to receive it. I claim this promise over my
finances today. Remove every financial barrier
and release Your supernatural provisions for
overflow. Open new streams of income and
sources of wealth that I have not
experienced in my life.*

*Bless the works of my hands and cause me to
prosper. Give me favor with an abundance of
rich ideas, divine connections, the right people,
opportunities, investments, and resources for my
breakthrough. I come before You boldly asking
for my financial breakthrough. I have the faith
to receive my financial breakthrough. The Word
says You are both maker of the rich and
the poor. I will walk in abundance and be
a light in the world, proclaiming that
You God are the source of my blessings.*

*In your name, Jesus, I ask for discernment
regarding my finances so I can maximize every
opportunity you unveil in my life. Lead me in
the way that I should go to access my overflow.
Reveal to me creative ideas and innovations that
will lead to greater levels of prosperity. Where
I have sown in faith, allow me to reap a harvest
of tremendous financial increase. No matter the
current financial environment, cover me at all
times and make a way for me in the wilderness.
Father, let the blessings flow like water
even in the desert.*

*Lord, I surrender control of my finances to
You. Forgive me for any doubt, lack of trust,
vagabond, financial misdeeds, misaligned
financial priorities, debt, bondage, and
disobedience to your will.*

*Father, I ask that you grant me the wisdom to
properly manage my finances to align with a
divine strategy in being a good steward with
what you've entrusted to me. I reject get-rich-
quick schemes and choose to abide by your
principles of hard work, diligence, discipline,
and integrity. Surround me with wise
counsel to further assist me in realizing
this financial breakthrough.*

*I pray that in Your mercy, you would lift up
families in desperate need of a financial
breakthrough and provide for all who are
struggling to make ends meet. I pray that
you would fix disparities caused by racism,
prejudice, and discrimination that result in
unjust treatment in income equality, lending
practices, and asset accumulation.
Break down barriers for economic
advancements and abundance.*

*I declare no weapon formed against me shall
prosper as I retrieve my financial inheritance
in Christ. Lead me into a place of wealth and
happiness as the blessings of the Lord maketh
rich and addeth no sorrow with it. All this is
asked in the name of Christ Jesus, Amen!*

Postscript Essays

THE POSTSCRIPT ESSAYS were written to provide additional detail on the spiritual aspects of the book's content that may not fit neatly into the financial advisory text and to expound on some of the revelations that provide divine guidance. It also provides a place for messaging that challenges pre-consumed narratives about the people of the Bible.

In manufacturing, "pre-consumption" refers to the material or waste generated during production before a product reaches the customer. In a similar way, some of the cultural and theological "waste" we inherit—misinterpretations, myths, and distortions—gets presented as truth. These essays seek to strip away those distortions, exposing how the conflation of religion, mythology, and historical fact can be used to mislead.

I use this section to offer spiritual encouragement while addressing some of the harsh realities that affect our everyday lives. Sometimes, we call on the Lord, and it feels like everything is falling apart. The journey may start to feel unbearable, yet we yearn for God's presence in our lives, asking for help. God makes it known that He is with us despite these challenges. These essays remind us that God is always with us—even in hardship—and that not every challenge is financial in nature. Yet, when finances are involved, the weight of the conflict can feel especially heavy.

Time

N TIME (PAST, PRESENT, AND FUTURE) BY WISDOM, understanding, and knowledge, God created (established, designed, founded) the Heaven (length, width, depth) and the Earth (solid, liquid, gas).

In physics, the formula for time equals distance divided by velocity. Mathematically, the definition of the Equation of Time (E) is expressed as E = GHA (apparent Sun) – GHA (mean Sun), where GHA stands for Greenwich Hour Angle. The GHA is used because it is based on the Prime Meridian (PM), set at 0 degrees longitude, and serves as the reference point that divides the east from the west. Simply put, it refers to the angle at which the Sun is positioned in the sky at a given time, as indicated by a clock. Astronomers and scientists use this equation to precisely determine the time based on the Sun's position, especially when studying a celestial phenomenon. The position of the Sun has a direct relationship to how we measure time.

However, at creation, in the beginning, or at the start, time (past, present, and future) means so much more than these definitions interpreted and redefined in the flesh. To understand time as the creator, we must know the power and definition of time in the spirit. By definition, the future is a period following the moment of speaking or writing. The past is the period before the moment of speaking or writing. Therefore, the present is the moment of speaking or writing.

In the order of POWER, the past, present, and future are explained with the following revelation as it relates to time. *"A man's belly shall be satisfied with the fruit of his mouth; and with the increase of his lips shall he be filled." – Proverbs 18:20*

"Death and life are in the power of the tongue: and they that love it shall eat the fruit thereof." – Proverbs 18:21

"A good man out of the good treasure of the heart bringeth forth good things: and an evil man out of the evil treasure bringeth forth evil things. But I say unto you, That every idle word that men shall speak, they shall give account thereof in the day of judgment. For by thy words thou shalt be justified, and by thy words thou shalt be condemned." – Matthew 12:35-37

The POWER is that you have complete control of your future. The only thing you need to do is speak it or write it, given *"death and life are in the power of the tongue."* The past is only the period before you speak your future into existence. This doesn't mean that you won't be held accountable for your past transgressions because Christ said, *"they shall give account thereof in the day of judgment."* However, being washed in the blood, you can move forward to speak or write your future.

Often, we are held back by the guilt of our past behaviors, not realizing that the past is only the moment before you speak or write your future. The enemy will claim access to your life by reminding you of that which was done prior to speaking your future. In dwelling on the past and not speaking your future, the enemy is given legal right to impact your life because you decided to think about what was done previously and not speak or write your future. Ask for forgiveness, acknowledge your sin, and speak or write your future to be freed.

The enemy will speak or write a future for you! The enemy will use every medium possible, whether music, television, cinema, news, reports, statistics, or writings, to give you the future they want. Speak or write your future. Do not consume the words or writings of the enemy. Take control of your future.

The Future is the period following the moment of speaking or writing your future into existence. *"And God said, Let there be light: and there was light." – Genesis 1:3*

"And God said, Let there be a firmament in the midst of the waters, and let it divide the waters from the waters. And God made the firmament, and divided the waters which were under the firmament from the waters which were above the firmament: and it was so." – Genesis 1:6-7

"And God said, Let the waters under the heaven be gathered together unto one place, and let the dry land appear: and it was so." – Genesis 1:9

The business plan is the process of writing your creation into existence. Take it seriously. Not writing your business plan inhibits its creation. Discuss your business and craft an effective elevator speech. Not speaking about the business you've created inhibits its creation. Speak positively about your abilities, your business, and your products. If there are deficiencies, bring their correction into existence by speaking positively about how things will be fixed. Then do it.

We often say that time is money. Here we are giving money all of the power. In doing so, we forfeit all of our power. As a creator, time is what you speak into existence. Meditate on what you want to bring into existence (past). Then write and speak what you want to bring into existence (present). Finally, do what you wrote and spoke (future)! This is your POWER in time (past, present, and future).

The Power Requires You to Believe

THE POWER WE HAVE IS IN THE TONGUE as we bring what we speak or write into existence. We cannot bring anything into existence if we lack faith and don't believe.

"And a certain woman, which had an issue of blood twelve years, And had suffered many things of many physicians, and had spent all that she had, and was nothing bettered, but rather grew worse, When she had heard of Jesus, came in the press behind, and touched his garment. For she said, If I may touch but his clothes, I shall be whole. And straightway the fountain of her blood was dried up; and she felt in her body that she was healed of that plague." – Mark 5:25-29

Jesus asked who had touched him, and the woman came and told him the truth. *"And he said unto her, Daughter, thy faith hath made thee whole; go in peace, and be whole of thy plague." – Mark 5:34.* The woman first spoke into existence that if she were to just touch his clothes, she would be cured. She was able to speak it into existence because she believed! She then touched his clothes. If the woman with the issue of blood did not believe she would be healed, then she would not have been able to access her power. This is why Christ says, Your faith is the reason you are healed.

"While he yet spake, there came from the ruler of the synagogue's house certain which said, Thy daughter is dead: why troublest thou the Master any further? As soon as Jesus heard the word that was spoken, he saith unto the ruler of the synagogue, Be not afraid, only believe. And he suffered no man to follow him, save Peter, and James, and John the brother of James. And he cometh to the house of the ruler of the synagogue, and seeth the tumult, and them that wept and wailed greatly. And when he was come in, he saith unto them, Why make ye this ado, and weep? the damsel is not dead, but sleepeth. And they laughed him to scorn. But when he had put them all out, he taketh the father and the mother of the damsel, and them that were with him, and entereth in where the damsel was lying. And he took the damsel by the hand, and said unto her, Talitha cumi; which is, being interpreted, Damsel, I say unto thee, arise. And straightway the damsel arose, and walked; for she was of the age of twelve years. And they were astonished with a great astonishment." – Mark 5:35-42

The moment the ruler was told that his daughter had died, Christ told the ruler, "Don't be afraid" and "BELIEVE!" After Christ got to the house, he needed to kick everyone out. Only the father, mother, and believers were allowed to re-enter the house. In your life, there may come a point when you will need to kick non-believers out of your house, your organizations, your businesses, your friendships, your marriage, and your movement. Jesus needed to kick everyone out of the house first. Then he walked back in the house with only the BELIEVERS. Only then was he able to speak into existence and command the girl to get up.

How many instances throughout your life has Christ removed family members, friends, partners, coworkers, and even removed you from your job so that you can live your destiny? He needed to remove these things so he could tell you to get up! The other people didn't believe in you. Next time, don't wait for the Holy Spirit; remove them yourself.

Surround yourself with believers who speak into existence everything that they do. Believe what you say and speak or write it into existence. REMOVE the nonbelievers.

"Is not this the carpenter, the son of Mary, the brother of James, and Joses, and of Juda, and Simon? and are not his sisters here with us? And they were offended at him. But Jesus said unto them, A prophet is not without honour, but in his own country, and among his own kin, and in his own house. And he could there do no mighty work, save that he laid his hands upon a few sick folk, and healed them. And he marvelled because of their unbelief. And he went round about the villages, teaching."
– Mark 6:3-6

At home, people are going to judge you for who you were and not accept your destiny and purpose. Christ was only able to do a few miracles because of the people's disbelief. The last thing the enemy wants is a community and nation of believers. The low-frequency diet, music, entertainment, habits, social constructs, teachings, schools and socioeconomics are designed to keep you from believing. Christ finally went to other villages to teach where there were believers. Recognize that being made in His likeness with Power requires you to believe.

Believe you will enter into a better financial circumstance. Believe you will get out of debt. Believe you will be blessed.

Believe you will run a successful business. Believe you will get a raise. Believe you will get a promotion. Believe you will find the perfect job. Believe God has your back. Believe you will obtain financial freedom. Believe you will do every good work and change the world. Believe that God will open the windows of heaven, and pour you out a blessing, that there shall not be room enough to receive it. BELIEVE!

Christianity is Socialism

*"But if any provide not for his own, and
specially for those of his own house, he hath
denied the faith, and is worse than an infidel." –
1Timothy 5:8*

Providing for one's own through socialism—which advocates that the means of production, distribution, and exchange be regulated by the people (a dirty word for its proponents)—on a small community level eliminates desperation and fear by providing sound financial advice, training, and support. "Power to the People."

We all want our neighborhoods to have high property values, low crime rates, and high literacy rates. Strong local economies help achieve this goal through the contributions of good governance, as well as strategic giving to social organizations and nonprofits in these local communities.

Creating a strong community through socialism has many financial benefits. The creation of local jobs supports small businesses that reinvest profits into the community through youth programs, recreation, adult education, mental health, and wellness programs. Shared resources bring light to financial opportunities. Additionally, a communal financial infrastructure is collaborative, helping to address economic challenges, fostering a sense of security, and promoting further community investment to strengthen economic stability.

Socialism, unfortunately, has many definitions, with some representing systems that have been used by oppressive governments. Merriam-Webster defines socialism as governmental ownership and administration of the means of production and distribution of goods, which is something none of us should agree with. Britannica Money defines socialism as a social and economic doctrine that calls for public rather than private ownership or control of property and natural resources. Accordingly, individuals do not work and live in isolation but in cooperation with one another. Everything the people produce is a social product where everyone who contributes to the production of a good is entitled to a share in it.

In reading the Bible, you will see that the values are more in line with community socialism, rather than neo-fascism, a far-right authoritarian ultranationalist political ideology characterized by dictatorial power, forcible suppression of opposition, and a strong regimentation of society and the economy. Having grown up in a capitalist society, I am what is defined as a social capitalist. An organization, or person, engages in social capitalism when it makes a profit and is, for all purposes, capitalist, but acts towards a social benefit in its end goal, product, hiring, investing, or production, even if it's a traditional for-profit company.

"When thou cuttest down thine harvest in thy field, and hast forgot a sheaf in the field, thou shalt not go again to fetch it: it shall be for the stranger, for the fatherless, and for the widow:

that the LORD thy God may bless thee in all the work of thine hands." – Deutoronomy 24:19-22

A strong financial network where trusted information is shared, mentorship is provided, and connections to many different industries are critical to your success. Access to opportunities, capital, resources, political connections, and collaboration will help you achieve better outcomes. None of this is possible if you don't have your house in order, with money saved for investment opportunities, or without a strong community.

Interestingly, while Venezuela is often cited as a negative example of socialism, countries like Finland or Denmark are rarely framed the same way. One likely reason is that they operate without the constant threat of economic warfare—such as coerced central bank debt, pressure from outside "jackals," or the looming risk of regime change for noncompliance; looking out for the independent best interest of the people and the country versus a willful harvest of natural, economic, intellectual, and human resources.

Diving further into the example of Venezuela, in the late 90s and early 2000s, Venezuela was experiencing an economic boom due to a global commodity "supercycle"—a prolonged period of high and rising prices of grain, metal, oil, and gas. However, President Nicholas Maduro, on April 27, 2008, stated that the original twelve tribes of Israel are not in power today, the current population are not authentic Jews, and created a geopolitical party attempting to colonize the world to steal riches and oppress all people.

Unfortunately, whether voluntarily or involuntarily, instead of employing the verse, *"Give a portion to seven, and also to*

eight; for thou knowest not what evil shall be upon the earth."
– *Ecclesiastes 11:2*, the government entered into double-digit deficits, spending more than its sources of revenue.

The central bank financed these unnecessary deficits with over $100 billion in obligations secured by the state-owned oil company and the government. Heavy reliance on the central bank printing money to finance deficits is highly inflationary, acting as a tax on savings and wages through higher consumer prices. The lack of adequate reinvestment in the oil industry, coupled with the replacement of technical experts with political allies, led to a significant decline in quality and production. Gains in lower-quality joint ventures with foreign oil companies initially hid oil production losses.

The domestic non-oil economy may have been crippled by self-destructive microeconomic policies where the government forcibly took control over the economy while being overtly hostile to private markets and private property.

Thousands of firms and several million hectares (1 hectare = 100 acres) of land were confiscated (nationalized) in agriculture, banking, cement, iron, oil, manufacturing, retail, and telecommunication, mostly without compensation.

The government then imposed capital controls and a byzantine system for foreign currency purchases. What does this mean exactly? To understand the negative reference to a convoluted and devious political administrative process, we will need to define what the Byzantine Empire involves.

The Byzantine Empire System refers to a complex government, society, and culture of the Eastern Roman Empire characterized by a highly centralized autocratic monarchy. The Byzantine emperor held supreme power, controlling the military, government, and church. A large number of judges, law firms, legal officials, and court administrators appointed by the emperor managed the empire's affairs. The government controlled the economy through heavy regulations and intimidation. Socially, citizens identified strongly as both Christians and Romans. The family structure was central and followed traditional hierarchies. The system is often inconsistent in information, messaging, direction, and results.

The Byzantine system for foreign currency is important because Venezuela's fiat currency declined significantly, forcing the government to resort to methods that would minimize the impact of inflation and exchange rates on imports. Businesses were unable to obtain access to the foreign currency necessary for operation. The government also set prices on retail goods by decree on everything from rice and chicken to soap and toilet paper. The price ceilings were set too low; therefore, producers could not cover their costs, leading to shortages, smuggling, and bankruptcies.

The government also capped profits with extremely harsh enforcement policies involving inventory seizures and jail time for workers and executives. These measures inhibited domestic production (farming, especially) and created a reliance on imports, even for previously exported products. In addition, the country lost over an estimated $300 billion to corruption through its foreign currency system and other financial schemes.

More central bank debt led to a 20%-30% monthly expansion of the money supply, pushing Venezuela into a hyperinflationary spiral where prices rose by 50% per month starting in

November 2017. Eventually, the country would default on its debt obligations. Next came sanctions and external pressure for regime change.

Presidents Chavez and Maduro captured and removed the country's democratic institutions, from the electoral authority to the military and media. Once the country became authoritarian, there was little that could be done beyond a revolution.

There are two possible arguments. Venezuela became the victim of neo-fascism, not socialism. Or, the Presidents were desperately attempting to protect the country from offshore economic colonization efforts.

"Is not this the fast that I have chosen? to loose the bands of wickedness, to undo the heavy burdens, and to let the oppressed go free, and that ye break every yoke? Is it not to deal thy bread to the hungry, and that thou bring the poor that are cast out to thy house? when thou seest the naked, that thou cover him; and that thou hide not thyself from thine own flesh? Then shall thy light break forth as the morning, and thine health shall spring forth speedily: and thy righteousness shall go before thee; the glory of the LORD shall be thy rereward." – Isaiah 58:6-8

Bedrock & Pillow Jams

"And when they had prayed, the place was shaken where they were assembled together; and they were all filled with the Holy Ghost, and they spake the word of God with boldness. And the multitude of them that believed were of one heart and of one soul: neither said any of them that ought of the things which he possessed was his own; but they had all things common." – Acts 4:31-32

The family decided to go to the town carnival, which is always a great experience. The carnival has a host of thrilling rides, plentiful food options, beer and wine, and live music. My wife invited our good friend, whose son is also our daughter's first-grade classmate, and his two siblings. The agreement was to meet at the carnival and leave after the 9 p.m. fireworks. My family got to the carnival around 6 p.m., which was plenty of time to enjoy all the festivities. After getting our ride tickets, we headed to the Spider-Man obstacle course. The obstacle course included wall climbing, pop-up obstacles, rope climbing, bridges, and a huge slide into a bouncing area at the end. My daughter loved it. Next was the Minecraft obstacle course. She was able to get through this one fairly quickly, so we decided to get food while waiting for our friends to arrive.

The food options at the carnival were of a willful good death. There was funnel cake, fried Oreos, tacos, empanadas, Cuban sandwiches, smash burgers, grilled kabobs, loaded fries, lemonade, beer, wine, and every sin imaginable. We sat at a table in front of the live band to consume bad cholesterol and diabetic pernicious cuisine.

After the meal, we headed to bumper cars, mega slides, and then the spinning cup ride. Our friends finally arrived, and the kids were off. We tried every ride that was considered reasonable for their ages. All of a sudden, it was 9 p.m. and the fireworks started. Only the adults were impressed. The kids couldn't care less and were only interested in getting on more rides. Off we went. I was able to see the fireworks from a distance while the kids were on the rides.

By 10:30 p.m., everyone was hungry again. We bought everything and shared it all. At least there was still a band playing, although it was different from when we sat down to eat earlier. My wife, being the life of the party, gladly participated in all of the shenanigans, even helping to sing a cover of *Valerie* on the microphone as the lead singer came off the stage and into the crowd. The band also came off the stage to give all of the kids tambourines to participate.

By midnight, we began to joke about our parenting decisions. The kids got on as many rides as they could, ate garbage, and danced the night away. With all shared resources depleted, my daughter came to me and said, "Daddy, we're going to start a band." Our friend, and mother of three, said, "The only band you're starting is Bedrock & Pillow Jams. It's time to go to bed!"

Money in Marriage

Making the Math Work

Marriage is the union between a man and a woman under the authority of God, witnessed by the community of family and friends. The Divine Math behind this equation is significant. It's interesting to hear married people speak of their spouse as the other half. This is not how the math works. God is a multiplier. Therefore, 0.5 times 0.5 is 0.25. This means that you are less in the union of marriage, based on divine multiplication, than when you are single. This type of marriage operates in dysfunction because most don't understand the simple math behind it.

As individuals, we are only made whole through Christ! We are unable to become whole on our own. This is how one whole person in Christ multiplied by one whole person in Christ becomes one union in marriage. If Christ is not at the center of the marriage, then you are unable to become one flesh.

"For this cause shall a man leave his father and mother, and shall be joined unto his wife, and they two shall be one flesh. This is a great mystery: but I speak concerning Christ and the church. Nevertheless, let every one of you in particular so love

his wife even as himself; and the wife see that she reverence her husband." – Ephesians 5:31-33

Husbands are to love their wives, and wives are to have a deep, profound respect for their husbands. When you are married, the ministerial officiant ends the ceremony with, "By the powers vested in me by the Almighty God, I now present to you Mr. & Mrs. Husband's First and Last Name." This is because you are now one flesh. If one of you is sick, you both are ill. If one of you is happy, you are both happy. If one of you gets a promotion, you both get a promotion. If one of you is hungry, you both are hungry. When you're talking to the husband, you're talking to the wife, even if she's not present. When the wife is speaking or when she is not with her husband, she is representing him as well.

This impacts how money is managed within a marriage. A selfish, me-first, and sometimes only-me society has conditioned individuals within marriage to fight or compete with each other, resulting in two individuals fighting over control. *"For no man ever yet hated his own flesh;"* – *Ephesians 5:29*

The pain it took for you to be molded into what God made you to be thus far is the same pain it will take for the marriage to become the representative of God on earth. Don't quit before you see the results of how God made you into one flesh. Those in marriages that have made it know how hard it is to constantly evolve as one. The continuous work required to grow matches the reward.

Here are a few tips on how to operate as one regarding your finances.

Prayer – When you and your spouse wake up every morning, the first thing you need to do is pray together. Give God praise for what He's done. Next, pray for covering over one another and your family. Finally, speak into existence what you are going to accomplish. Speak abundance over one another. Speak blessings into one another. Speak triumph over the day. Speak that every need will be met. When it's time to go to bed, pray together. Give God praise. Speak rejuvenation. Speak health, peace, rest, and recovery!

Build Trust – Start by setting aside time to communicate what you know and don't know about money. Educate one another about how you grew up, your experiences with money, and what type of lifestyle you want to live. Discuss the many sacrifices in time, effort, and money it will take to achieve these lifestyle goals. Create small financial goals, like paying off a credit card or starting a college savings account for your children. Build trust by accomplishing these small financial goals.

Wisdom & Instruction – Schedule time to learn something new about finance together. Create a list of financial books to read. Share articles from financial websites to discuss. Spend a few minutes watching financial news together. Continue to learn about money. Become so in tune that when one partner reads a financial book, they can communicate its concepts in a manner that their spouse can easily receive. Therefore, after reading the same book and discussing it with your spouse, learn how your spouse receives and understands information. The next step is to read different financial books separately and discuss and explain the content to one another. This force multiplier strategy increases speed and capacity.

Create a Plan – Once you have financial goals, develop a budget that reflects both parties' income, expenses, and financial obligations. Agree to monthly spending limits on discretionary expenses. Have a joint savings plan. Identify where the savings and investments are going. Build an Emergency Fund!

Wise Financial Counsel – Wise counsel will help you build a strong foundation for a shared and often complex financial future together. Trusted financial counsel will help married couples identify their risk tolerance, provide a strategy for working through competing ideas to find common ground, and help build a mutually beneficial financial future.

Financial Infidelity

Financial infidelity is when a spouse deliberately hides the truth about money and debt. Financial infidelity covers a wide range of money-related lies, including: hiding income by placing funds into a secret bank account; hiding purchases; secretly draining a joint bank account and depositing those funds into a secret account; lending out money without the knowledge or consent of the other spouse; and lying about income, whether it be the amount or source.

Most people show signs of financial infidelity in many ways. If you start noticing large packages in the mail or intercept the delivery of an item, this is an important time to discuss spending habits. Some spouses may hide new purchases and even find ways to secretly discard the packaging. While reviewing bank statements, you may notice charges that don't make sense or that you were unaware of. Collections notices or statements from banks with unfamiliar accounts are an obvious sign. If a spouse is nervous about what's in their electronic devices or gets upset if you want to see their phone, this may be a sign.

It's essential to take the necessary steps to resolve financial issues and begin to practice group economics. Marital financial success requires trust, a shared mission, and cooperation. Financial compatibility may not be perfect in the beginning. However, with financial purpose, improved daily communication, and a joint financial plan, you can achieve your financial goals.

Reinforcements

"In the third year of Cyrus king of Persia a thing was revealed unto Daniel, whose name was called Belteshazzar; and the thing was true, but the time appointed was long: and he understood the thing, and had understanding of the vision.

In those days I Daniel was mourning three full weeks.

I ate no pleasant bread, neither came flesh nor wine in my mouth, neither did I anoint myself at all, till three whole weeks were fulfilled.

And in the four and twentieth day of the first month, as I was by the side of the great river, which is Hiddekel;

Then I lifted up mine eyes, and looked, and behold a certain man clothed in linen, whose loins were girded with fine gold of Uphaz:

His body also was like the beryl, and his face as the appearance of lightning, and his eyes as lamps of fire, and his arms and his feet like in colour to polished brass, and the voice of his words like the voice of a multitude.

And I Daniel alone saw the vision: for the men that were with me saw not the vision; but a great quaking fell upon them, so that they fled to hide themselves.

Therefore I was left alone, and saw this great vision, and there remained no strength in me: for my comeliness was turned in me into corruption, and I retained no strength.

Yet heard I the voice of his words: and when I heard the voice of his words, then was I in a deep sleep on my face, and my face toward the ground.

And, behold, an hand touched me, which set me upon my knees and upon the palms of my hands.

And he said unto me, O Daniel, a man greatly beloved, understand the words that I speak unto thee, and stand upright: for unto thee am I now sent. And when he had spoken this word unto me, I stood trembling.

Then said he unto me, Fear not, Daniel: for from the first day that thou didst set thine heart to understand, and to chasten thyself before thy God, thy words were heard, and I am come for thy words.

But the prince of the kingdom of Persia withstood me one and twenty days: but, lo, Michael, one of the chief princes, came to help me; and I remained there with the kings of Persia.

Now I am come to make thee understand what shall befall thy people in the latter days: for yet the vision is for many days.

And when he had spoken such words unto me, I set my face toward the ground, and I became dumb.

And, behold, one like the similitude of the sons of men touched my lips: then I opened my mouth, and spake, and said unto him that stood before me, O my lord, by the vision my sorrows are turned upon me, and I have retained no strength.

For how can the servant of this my lord talk with this my lord? for as for me, straightway there remained no strength in me, neither is there breath left in me.

Then there came again and touched me one like the appearance of a man, and he strengthened me,

And said, O man greatly beloved, fear not: peace be unto thee, be strong, yea, be strong. And when he had spoken unto me, I was strengthened, and said, Let my lord speak; for thou hast strengthened me.

Then said he, Knowest thou wherefore I come unto thee? and now will I return to fight with the prince of Persia: and when I am gone forth, lo, the prince of Grecia shall come.

But I will show thee that which is noted in the scripture of truth: and there is none that holdeth with me in these things, but Michael your prince." – Daniel 10

The reason that your blessing has not come to you in the instance that it was requested is because the enemy is fighting to prevent the fulfillment of your blessings. The angel of the LORD told Daniel that the prince of Persia withstood him for 21 days. This means that a fight occurred between the demon who was in charge of the region and the angel, where the demon (prince) managed to prevent the angel from delivering the message to Daniel.

The king of Persia was introduced in Daniel 10:1. The prince, who withstood the angel, is introduced in Daniel 10:13. The angel was only able to deliver the message after the Archangel Miki-EL (Michael), described as one of God's chief princes, came to fight. The angel says he and the Archangel remained there to fight with the kings of Persia. This suggests there were even more powerful adversaries that came to join the fight. The fight involved Miki-EL, the angel delivering the divine message, the kings of Persia (multiple powerful demons), and the prince of Persia. The angel, speaking to Daniel, said, *"Now I am come to make thee understand."*

Sometimes, you will need reinforcements to fulfill God's purpose. You are not alone. Ask God for help through prayer so He can send you people with financial wisdom or experience that is specific to your needs.

The passage of scripture states that Heaven heard Daniel's request as soon as it was made. The passages said that the angel was sent immediately to deliver the message so that Daniel would understand. Yet, the delay was the result of warfare.

Daniel was exhausted! His countenance, comeliness, health, and strength were almost depleted. If you've ever been on the verge of a financial breakthrough, you will feel like there's so much going on that's impeding your success. The number of distractions that will come against you may be enormous. The old sins, people, stimuli, or lusts return from the past to tempt you when you've already moved past them. Acknowledge the past with the acceptance that you've moved on, no longer affected by the past. They will allow for a release, as God is removing everything at this level so He can elevate you to the next! No grudges! No resentment! Be at peace!

Put down the unwanted stress or confusion about why you can't move forward. It feels like you're right on the cusp of entering into your new season of overflow, but can't quite get over the mountain. This is because of the fight going on in the spiritual realm. Remember to first believe it's already accomplished. Then walk in the truth that permeates from within your inner spirit, which will bring all things into the physical realm.

After the angel delivers the message to Daniel, he explains that since you know from whence I came, who I was fighting, where the battle took place, and how I was able to prevail, I must go back to fight! The angel proceeds to explain that after I defeat the prince of Persia, another will come. The angel assures Daniel that there is none mightier nor able to defeat God's chief prince, Archangel Miki-EL. The chief prince, Archangel Miki-EL, "Who is like God," was able to fight the kings of Persia and the prince of Persia, allowing the message to be delivered. Continue to pray, fast, praise God, be thankful, and read the Word. When the message is delivered, take immediate action. I encourage you to FIGHT! The manifestation of your inner acceptance of being successful, rich, wealthy, and living in abundance is on its way. The physical world is delayed. The physical reality is only a reflection of what you've already imagined, spoken, written, and decided to accept in the spirit. Walk in faith as the person you've already decided to become. Everything will be added as a result.

Identity Economics & The Slander, Libel, Manipulation, Propaganda, and Defamation of Ham

*The **dissonance** between what we are told and what we see with our own eyes.*

RADITIONAL ECONOMICS is a social science that focuses on the production, distribution, and consumption of goods and services. Economics, as a discipline, analyzes the choices individuals, businesses, and governments make to allocate limited resources.

Identity Economics integrates social and psychological factors that are considered powerful motivators, oftentimes even more than strictly financial motivations. Our identity can significantly impact economic decisions as social norms, family influences, and community environments dictate our level of education, career paths, consumption habits, savings habits, and group economics.

Early Examples of Black Identity Economics in the United States

For several decades in the late 1800s, Blacks achieved enormous success in the port city of Wilmington, North Carolina. African Americans worked as professionals, artisans, and industrial workers. Between 1870 and 1880, Black businessmen and entrepreneurs amassed significant wealth, rivaling their white counterparts. This access to wealth helped Blacks gain political power, which they used to influence government.

The more financial capital and political influence Black residents gained, the angrier and more indignant white residents grew. In the November 8, 1898, election, a white mob forced the resignation of the city's mayor and removed Black employees from their municipal positions. Hundreds of Black community members were killed, and over 2,100 Black residents were forced to flee. At least 1,500 homes, previously owned by Blacks, were appropriated by whites.

The achievements of African Americans in the early 1900s, Tulsa, Oklahoma as an example, made Black people vulnerable to attacks. Visibly successful Black people, or towns that exemplified Black prosperity, triggered economic envy from whites.

"A glistening city-within-a-city, Greenwood was home to grocery and retail stores, theaters, restaurants and hotels—all the businesses and services that would cater to Black residents of a segregated state. Greenwood's streets were lined with stately mansions of doctors and business tycoons as well as the more modest dwellings of domestic workers. It was so prosperous that it became known as "Negro Wall Street.""

On May 21, 1921, a white mob descended on the city's prosperous Black enclave of Greenwood and bombed, looted, and destroyed 35 city blocks, killing over 300 people.

The CNN article *Burned from the land: How 60 years of racial violence shaped America*, states, "Between the end of the Civil War and the 1940s, the destruction seen in Tulsa happened in various ways to communities of color across the country. These acts of racial violence took aim at the roots of generational wealth, shaping the nation and its inequalities in ways we see today."

Eminent Domain

Eminent domain is the power of the government or its agent to take private property and expropriate it for public use, even if the owner doesn't want to sell, with just compensation. However, "just compensation" to property owners was never fair compensation, as the government never paid market value.

Eminent domain was another tool used to destroy communities of color in the name of urban renewal. Eminent domain began in the 1940s, and its net effect resulted in the displacement and disruption of many African American communities.

African American communities were the primary targets where highways, government properties, sports arenas, and parks replaced economically viable areas. Once a town was identified, the government gave residents three weeks to vacate the properties that were soon to be confiscated. Systematic racial segregation through Jim Crow, followed by Reconstruction, and redlining was characterized by laws designed to subjugate Black citizens to prevent them from building wealth.

Landlords would not rent to African Americans in certain neighborhoods, making it difficult to find suitable housing, especially within the required time frame. People lost their homes and personal belongings because there was no place to store these items.

African American Churches, which are the staple of the community, with some built in the 1800s, were demolished. Gas and oil companies, construction companies, cement plants, coal yards, brick yards, and various businesses were closed. The owners of these companies lost their businesses, and employees of the companies were now out of work, having devastating effects on the local Black economy.

Hotels, rooming houses, barber shops, repair shops, clothing stores, grocery stores, restaurants, and catering businesses all closed. The construction sites, brick yards, cement plants, and coal yards did not have cafeterias, so women provided catering services to these locations. As a result of urban renewal, these catering businesses lost their clientele, forcing them out of business.

The government paid what they deemed "just compensation" for the land and improvements. Just compensation is whatever the government deems appropriate, which was far below market value. The government didn't pay for the loss of income. The government didn't pay for moving expenses. Unfortunately, if you were a rentor, you got absolutely nothing.

Out of all that was lost, the most significant was the loss of community! During segregation, Black people could not go to any white businesses or neighborhoods for their needs. Through eminent domain, Blacks were completely shut out economically. We could replace the items lost. However, we were never able to replace the economic community. The Black economic community needed one another to provide all the required necessities. Even when Black people could eventually find a place to stay locally or in another state, the effects of a torn community remained.

The House of Representatives reported that, at its peak in the mid-1960s, urban renewal displaced approximately 66,000 families annually. When the Civil Rights Movement secured voting rights and the desegregation of public and private spaces, the federal government responded by using eminent domain to clear out entire Black neighborhoods. Federal subsidies displaced over 1.2 million people; the overwhelming majority were African Americans.

Propagandistic mechanisms used to project labels of Black ineptitude, Black illegitimacy, and Black criminality were perpetuated in every medium. External efforts to superimpose environments that mirrored such biases were both violent and well-funded. All were elements of strategic economic warfare. There is no segment of the population in the U.S. or across the globe that has endured more physical and economic violence than Blacks.

All other communities, outside of the Black community, including Asian, Indian, White, and Hispanic, were able to build economic communities. This promoted the narrative that the African American Community had a cultural pathology. Add in the economic impact of the influx of narcotics coupled with the "War on Drugs" which ushered in *The New Jim Crow,* written by Michelle Alexander, prison-for-profit system, it's a miracle Black economics exists at all.

Today, stories of Black families needing to hire white people to pretend to be the homeowner when selling their property to get a fair appraisal or sales price are heavily documented. Economic violence is a perpetual experience that helps explain the racial wealth gap.

Malice

The first five books of the Torah (the Law) and the Holy Bible include Genesis, Exodus, Leviticus, Numbers, and Deuteronomy. What most don't know is that the Book of Genesis was the last of these first five books to be written.

"And the LORD spake unto Moses and unto Aaron, saying, When ye be come into the land of Canaan, which I give to you for a possession, and I put the plague of leprosy in a house of the land of your possession;" – Leviticus 14:33-34

Since Genesis was the last book written, it's easy to understand the predictive prejudice regarding the prophecy of the curse, which includes a plague and subordination, as well as the foretelling of taking possession of the land. *"Cursed be Canaan"* – *Genesis 9:25*. The reasons why the Israelites would have spoken so disparagingly about the Canaanites are because of the war between the Israelites and Canaanites, which lasted for several years and is detailed in the Book of Judges, in addition to a plague of leprosy that affected the land of Canaan described in Leviticus.

"And Noah began to be an husbandman, and he planted a vineyard: And he drank of the wine, and was drunken; and he was uncovered within his tent. And Ham, the father of Canaan,

*saw the nakedness of his father, and told his two brethren
without. And Shem and Japheth took a garment, and laid it
upon both their shoulders, and went backward, and covered the
nakedness of their father; and their faces were backward, and
they saw not their father's nakedness. And Noah awoke from his
wine, and knew what his younger son had done unto him. And
he said, Cursed be Canaan; a servant of servants shall he be
unto his brethren." – Genesis 9:20-25*

It's easy to deduce from the scripture that Noah was upset
with his younger son, and upon waking up, he cursed one of
his grandsons, Canaan. Noah had several grandsons who
represented different African Nations outlined in Genesis.
*"And the sons of Ham; Cush (Ethiopia), and Mizraim (Egypt),
and Phut (Libya), and Canaan (Israel, Palestine, Lebanon)."*
– Genesis 10:6

An important continuation of this lineage is that of Cush. Cush
birthed the nations of Seba (Sudan), and Havilah (Arabia), and
Sabtah (Southern Coast of Arabia), and Raamah (Oman, United
Arab Emirates), and Sabtechah (Somalia). What you will find
is that some of those same regions, which will be described as
having the lineage of Shem, were first Hamitic.

Francois Lenormant, French Hellenist, Assyriologist, and
archeologist, wrote in his book *The Origin of the Chaldaio-
Babylonian Cosmogonies* that the famous Ethiopians or
Kushites of Babylon ruled. Citing scripture, he explained that
the Kushites, the descendants of Nimrod (Mesopotamia, Sumer,
Sumerian, Saudi Arabia, Iraq, Babel, Babylon), were "the most
ancient Babylonians."

The Sumerians called themselves the "Black-Headed," while
the Egyptians called themselves the "Black-Footed".

"And Cush begat Nimrod: he began to be a mighty one in the earth. He was a mighty hunter before the LORD: wherefore it is said, Even as Nimrod the mighty hunter before the LORD. And the beginning of his kingdom was Babel (Babylon), and Erech (Southeastern Iraq), and Accad (Northern Mesopotamia, Bagdad), and Calneh (Northern Iraq), in the land of Shinar (Mesopotamia / Modern Day Iraq)." – Genesis 10:8-10

The misstatement that Ham is the younger/youngest is disproved through the recording of history, anthropology, DNA genomes, ancient literature, and archeology. Genesis 10:8-10 details the lineage quite accurately despite this misstatement.

Could this be a minor misstep in oral tradition, which was passed down for centuries, possibly thousands of years, before any texts were created? Oral tradition is important because of its role in shaping content, influencing stories, and interpreting texts.

Is it an attempt to marry the mythology of storytelling to factual historical information? Or were texts rewritten, reordered, rearranged, and possibly manipulated at the Council of Nicaea, convened by the Roman Emperor Constantine in 325 AD?

Perhaps institutionalized deception or purposeful miseducation occurred during the construction of the King James version, published in 1611. Who knows for certain? The Ethiopian Bible, specifically the Garima Gospels, is the oldest complete illustrated Christian manuscript. The Ethiopian Bible contains an additional 29 books (88 in total) compared to 66 books in the later revised versions published under King James. This passage within the Ethiopian Bible, though worded differently and providing a bit more instruction, has the same account. Read the Book of Enoch I and II in the Ethiopian Bible for perspective.

"These are the generations of Noah: Noah was a just man and perfect in his generations, and Noah walked with God. And Noah begat three sons, Shem, Ham, and Japheth." – Genesis 6:9-10

Japheth represents the areas of Europe, including Greece, the Aegean Sea, Turkey, Italy, Russia, Germany, and Asia Minor. *"The sons of Japheth; Gomer (Southern Russia, Turkey, Armenia), and Magog (Kazakhstan, Kyrhyzstan, Ubekistan, Turkmenistan, Tajikistan, and parts of Afghanistan), and Madai (Iran), and Javan (Greece), and Tubal (modern day Turkey), and Meshech (Asia Minor / Turkey), and Tiras (Southeast Europe)." – Genesis 10:2*

Gomer's descendants are sometimes referred to as "Beyond the Caucasus." *"And the sons of Gomer; Ashkenaz (Germany), and Riphath (Asia Minor), and Togarmah (Eastern Turkey and the Caucasus)."* – Genesis 10:3

"Unto Shem also, the father of all the children of Eber (Assyria – northern Iraq, southeastern Turkey, northeastern Syria, and northwest Iran), the brother of Japheth the elder, even to him were children born." – Genesis 10:21

"The children of Shem; Elam (Northwest Iran), and Asshur (Northeastern Syria, Northern Iraq, Southeast Turkey), and Arphaxad (Assyria, Northern Iran), and Lud (Eastern Turkey near Greece), and Aram (Syria, Northeast Iraq)." – Genesis 10:22

Somehow, the passage changes from Shem, Ham, and Japheth to this line in scripture, describing Japheth as the oldest! Where did this come from? Europe becomes the older brother of Shem (Iraq, Iran, Arabia, Mesopotamia, Persia – Northeast Africa & 20th century "Middle East") and Ham (Africa, Alkebu-Lan, Mother of Mankind, Eden, Ethiopia, Kemet, Egypt, Libya, and Canaan, Palestine, Lebanon).

The Africans taught the Greeks, who referred to the region of Ham as "Divine" or "The Land of the Gods" due to the sophistication of its civilization, advancements in medicine, agriculture, wisdom, libraries, economy, and institutions. The Greeks taught the Romans. Yet, the lineage in the passage somehow exalts Europe as the oldest!

"But now they that are younger than I have me in derision, Whose fathers I would have disdained to have set with the

dogs of my flock. Yea, whereto might the strength of their hands profit me, In whom old age was perished? For want and famine they were solitary; Fleeing into the wilderness in former time desolate and waste. Who cut up mallows by the bushes, And juniper roots for their meat. They were driven forth from among men, (They cried after them as after a thief;) To dwell in the cliffs of the valleys, in caves of the earth, and in the rocks. Among the bushes they brayed; Under the nettles they were gathered together. They were children of fools, yea, children of base men: They were viler than the earth. And now am I their song, Yea, I am their byword (racial epithet)." – *Job 30:1-9*

No wonder Europe is the oldest, wisest, and blessed with beauty, "God doth give beauty to Japheth", while the youngest brother, Ham (Africa), who taught the world everything and is the "Mother of Mankind", is cursed. This is not a coincidence.

If you can control the narrative, you control the money. Justification of Europe's theft of Africa's land, minerals, and natural resources all started with the indoctrination of a lie, "The Curse of Ham". Colonialism needs propaganda. "Use their religion and culture against them."

In the text, Noah curses Canaan, but we've been institutionalized to believe God curses Ham. So, even when reading the passage out loud, *"And Noah awoke from his wine, and knew what his younger son had done unto him, And he said, Cursed be Canaan; a servant of servants shall he be unto his brethren,"* our brains immediately revert to this programming and vomit out that God cursed Ham. Yet, this is 1000% untrue. God is not mentioned nor involved. God sees all but has not intervened.

"Yea, and all that will live godly in Christ Jesus shall suffer

persecution. But evil men and seducers shall wax worse and worse, deceiving, and being deceived. But continue thou in the things which thou hast learned and hast been assured of, knowing of whom thou hast learned them; And that from a child thou hast known the holy scriptures, which are able to make thee wise unto salvation through faith which is in Christ Jesus." – *2 Timothy 3:12-15*

"All scripture is given by inspiration of God, and is profitable for doctrine, for reproof, for correction, for instruction in righteousness: That the man of God may be perfect, thoroughly furnished unto all good works." – *2 Timothy 3:16-17*

When Christ came into the world blameless, removing all sins, curses, or disobedience, Jesus gave every person and nation a clean slate. Therefore, not only are people continuing to perpetrate a lie, but they are also actively participating in a system to exercise a proclaimed legal right that Christ eliminated on Calvary. So, even if you believed the lie, there is still NO LEGAL RIGHT after Christ!

Old Maps

1584 map

Ortelius, Abraham,1527-1598.

"Africae tabula noua." Copperplate map, with added color, 37 x 49 cm. From Ortelius's *Theatrum orbis terrarum* (Antwerp, 1584). [Historic Maps Collection]

1644 map

Blaeu, Willem Janszoon, 1571-1638.

"Africae nova descriptio." Copperplate *carte à figures* map, with added color, 35 x 45 cm. From the second volume of Blaeu's *Le theatre dv monde; ov Novvel atlas contenant les chartes et descriptions de tous les païs de la terre* (Amsterdam, 1644). Gift of J. Monroe Thorington, Class of 1915. [Rare Books Division]

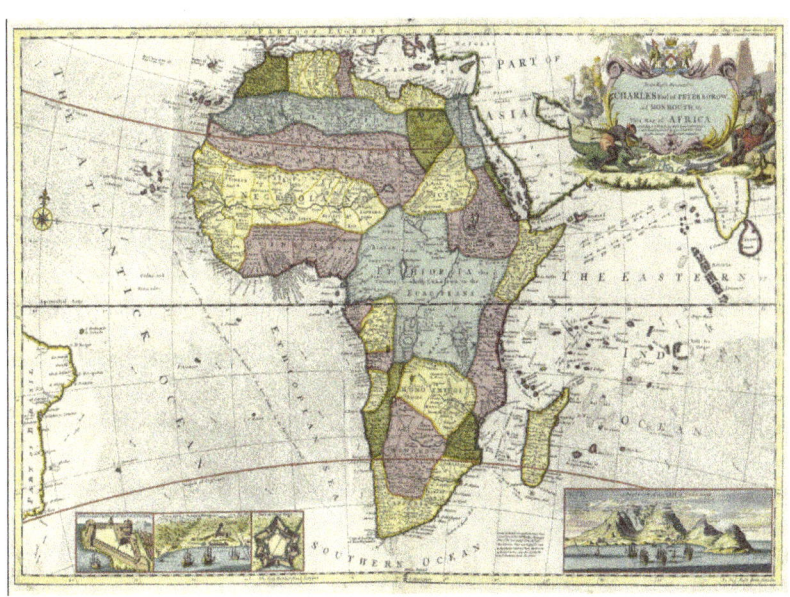

1710 map

Moll, Herman, d. 1732.

"To the Right Honourable Charles, Earl of Peterborow and Monmouth, &c This Map of Africa . . . Is Most Humbly Dedicated." Copperplate map, with added color, 56 x 94 cm. [Historic Maps Collection]

1737 map

Hase, Johann Matthias, 1684-1742.

"Africa secundum legitimas projectionis stereographicae regulas et juxta recentissimas relationes et observationes in subsidium vocatis quoque veterum Leonis Africani. . . ." Copperplate map, with added color, 45 x 57 cm. [Historic Maps Collection]

Glossary

401(k) plan – A flexible retirement plan for businesses with employees. Investors in the plan don't have to pay taxes on the income they invest until they withdraw the funds at retirement age.

529 Plan – A program set up to allow an adult to either prepay or contribute to an account established for paying a student's qualified education expenses at an eligible educational institution.

Account – A banking service allowing a customer's money to be handled and tracked. Common bank accounts are savings and checking accounts.

Adjustable-rate mortgage (ARM) – A loan that allows the lender to make changes in the interest rate, and the resulting principal and interest payments charged to the borrower. These rate changes are usually tied to the rise and fall of a financial statistic (called an index), such as the Secured Overnight Financing Rate (SOFR), prime rate, or Treasury Bill rate. The initial interest rate on ARMs is lower than rates on fixed-rate mortgages, as the borrower is taking the risk of the interest rate rising over time. The borrower is protected by a maximum interest rate, which the lender may reset annually. There may be a limit on the number and amount of increases or decreases to the interest rate at each change date or over the life of the loan.

Annual fee – The fee a credit card company charges a credit card holder to use the card for a year. Or, the fee a lender charges a borrower for the use of a line of credit for a year.

Annual percentage rate (APR) – A measurement used to compare different loans, the APR takes into account a loan's interest rate, term, and fees to illustrate the total cost of credit expressed as a yearly rate. The lower the APR, the lower the total cost of the loan.

Annual percentage yield (APY) – The rate of return on an investment, such as a deposit in an interest-bearing savings account, for a one-year period.

Appraisal – A professional estimate of a property's market value.

Appreciation – The amount of value an item, such as a stock or a home, gains over time from the original purchase price.

Asset – Anything of value owned by a person or company. For example, a person's assets might include cash, a house, a car, and stocks. A business's assets might include cash, equipment, and inventory.

Bad credit – A situation in which lenders believe that, due to a borrower's poor history of repaying his or her debts, further loans to this person would be especially risky.

Balloon payment – A final lump sum payment that is due, often at the maturity date of a balloon mortgage.

Bank – A financial institution that handles money, including keeping it for saving or commercial purposes, and exchanging, investing, and supplying it for loans.

Bankruptcy – To legally declare yourself unable to repay your debts. A bankruptcy remains on a person's credit history for up to seven years. Depending on the type of bankruptcy, it could stay on a person's credit history for up to ten years.

Bond – An investment offered to the public by a corporation, the U.S. Government, or a city. A bond pays interest annually and is payable in full at a specified date. Bonds are rated, and the rating indicates their probability of default.

Budget – An estimate of income and expenditures for a set period of time.

Capital gain – The dollar amount by which an asset's selling price exceeds its initial purchase price. For example, if you buy a stock for $4 per share and sell it for $7 per share, your capital gain is $3 per share.

Capital loss – The decrease in value of an investment or asset. The opposite of capital gain.

Certificates of Deposit – A bank account in which you agree to keep the money in the bank for a specified period of time, usually anywhere from three months to several years. As a result, this account usually offers higher rates of return than a savings account. Money removed before the agreed-upon date is subject to an early withdrawal penalty. The account pays interest on the deposit and is

FDIC-insured. Banks issue an actual certificate for a CD account. If no certificate is issues, the account is known instead as a "time deposit".

Closing – The day and time when all final mortgage documents are signed and all necessary payments are transferred to complete the purchase of a house. Also known as the settlement date.

Closing costs – Expenses or settlement costs, above the home sales price, charged to both the buyer and seller to complete the transfer of the property in connection with obtaining a mortgage loan. There are also closing costs on a refinance loan.

Collateral – Any asset of a borrower (for example, a home) that a lender has a right to take ownership of if the borrower doesn't repay the loan as agreed.

Collection agency – A business that specializes in collecting past due debts.

Compound interest – When a financial institution pays you interest not only on your initial principal (the amount you originally deposited) but also on the interest your deposit has earned over time.

Co-sign – A second person who signs your credit or loan application. Just like the borrower, the co-signer on a loan is equally responsible for repaying the debt. Also called a co-borrower.

Credit – When a bank or business allows its customers to purchase goods or services on the promise of future payment. Also used to describe any item that increases the balance in a bank account. Deposits and interest payments are both examples of credits.

Credit bureau – A company that gathers information on consumers who use credit. These companies send this information to lenders and other businesses in the form of a credit report. The three largest bureaus are Equifax, Experian, and TransUnion. The private companies are also known as credit reporting agencies or consumer reporting agencies.

Credit check – A lender, landlord, employer, or insurer's inquiry at a credit bureau for the purpose of evaluating the credit history of an applicant.

Credit counselor – A professional advisor who specializes in helping people with debt and credit problems.

Credit history – A written record of a person's use of credit, including applying for credit and using credit or loans to make purchases. Also called a credit record.

Credit limit – The maximum dollar amount the lender is willing to make available to the borrower according to the agreement between them. For example, if you have a credit card, the agreement will usually specify the maximum amount of money you're allowed to charge.

Credit rating – An evaluation of an individual's or business's financial history and the ability to pay debts. Lenders use this information to decide whether to approve a loan. The credit rating is usually in the form of a number or letter.

Credit record – Also known as your credit history, when provided by a credit bureau to a lender or other business.

Credit report – A report issued by an independent credit agency that contains information concerning a loan applicant's credit history and current credit standing.

Credit score (FICO) – A numerical rating that indicates an individual's creditworthiness based on a number of criteria. Credit scores are used by lenders in the loan approval decision process. (FICO).

Credit Union – A non-profit financial institution that is owned and operated entirely by its members. Credit unions provide financial services for their members, including savings and lending. Large organizations may organize credit unions for their members, and some companies establish credit unions for their employees. To join a credit union, a person must ordinarily belong to a participating organization, such as a college alumni association or labor union. When a person deposits money in a credit union, he or she becomes a member of the union because the deposit is considered partial ownership in the credit union.

Creditworthiness – A lender's measure of an individual or company's ability to pay debt.

Debit card – A card linked to a checking account that can be used to withdraw money and make deposits at an ATM and to make purchases at merchants. When you use a debit card, the money will be deducted from the linked checking account.

Debt – Money, goods, or services you owe to others.

Debt-to-income ratio – A percentage that is calculated by dividing a loan applicant's total debt payments by her gross income.

Default – Failure to repay a credit agreement according to its terms.

Defined Benefit Plan – A corporate retirement plan that pays employees a fixed retirement benefit either as a lump sum or as a pension (a lifetime payment). Payments are determined by salary earned and length of employment.

Defined contribution plan – A corporate retirement plan, such as a 401(k) or 403(b), where employees defer a percentage of their salaries and invest for retirement.

Deposit – to put money into an account

Depreciation – A loss of value in real property, or another asset, brought about by age, physical deterioration, functional or economic obsolescence.

Discretionary expenses – The purchase of goods or services that are not essential to the buyer, or are more expensive than necessary. Examples include entertainment and restaurant meals.

Diversification – An investing strategy designed to reduce risk by combining a variety of investments (such as stocks, bonds, and real estate). Having a variety of investments makes it less likely that all of them will move up and down at the same time or at the same rate.

Dividend – If a company does well financially, its board of directors may decide to pay a small amount of its profits, called a dividend, directly back to its shareholders. Dividends are usually cash, but may also take the form of stock or other property.

Down payment – A portion of the sales price paid to the seller by the homebuyer to close the sales transaction. Down payments usually range from 3% to 20% of the property value.

Educational Savings Account – An investment account designed to assist with paying for education-related expenses. Contributions grow tax-deferred, and distributions are not taxed if used for qualified expenses. Withdrawals for non-qualified educational expenses are subject to income tax and 10% IRS penalty. Distributions may be taxable.

Equity – The value of your investment above the total of your lien (debt).

Establishing credit – Giving lenders the trust and confidence to make loans to you based on a good history of paying your debts.

Estate – The net worth of an individual, including all of their assets.

Federal Deposit Insurance Corporation – An independent agency of the United States government that protects customers from the loss of their deposits if an FDIC-insured financial institution fails. The basic insurance amount is specified per depositor per insured financial institution. Certain retirement accounts, such as Individual Retirement Accounts, are insured up to specified amounts per depositor per insured financial institution. Customers can increase the amount of money insured at any one financial institution by owning deposit accounts in different ownership categories (e.g., Individual Accounts, Retirement Accounts, Joint Accounts, Revocable Trust Accounts). Please visit www.fdic.gov for the most current deposit insurance amounts.

Fees – Charges for services by a financial institution or lender

Finance charge – The amount of money a borrower pays to a lender for the privilege of borrowing money, including interest and other service charges.

Financial institution – Companies such as banks, credit unions, and savings institutions that provide a wide range of money management products and services to consumers. Financial institutions collect funds from the public and place them in financial assets, such as deposits, loans, and bonds.

Fixed expenses – For an individual, a fixed cost is an expense that stays the same each month, such as rent or a car payment. For a business, a fixed cost is an expense that does not vary depending on production or sales levels, such as an equipment lease or property tax.

Fixed rate – An interest rate that remains the same during the entire term of the loan.

Flexible expenses – An expense that you can control or adjust, for example, how much you spend on groceries, clothes, or entertainment.

Foreclosure – The legal process by which an owner's right to a property is terminated, usually because of failure to make loan payments as agreed. Foreclosure typically involves a forced sale of the property at public auction, with the money applied to the remaining debt.

Investing – Purchasing something of value (for example, stocks or real estate) with the goal of earning money over time if the value increases.

Landlord – The owner of a property that is leased or rented.

Late fees – The charge or fee that is added to a loan or credit card payment when the payment is made after the due date.

Lease – A contract by which one party (lessor) gives to another (lessee) the use and permission of an item, such as an automobile or apartment, for a specific time and fixed payments.

Lender, creditors – A business that makes money available for others to borrower.

Liability – The amount of money an individual or business owes to someone else; a debt.

Line of credit – An arrangement by which a lender extends a specific amount of credit to a borrower for a certain time period. As long as the borrower repays the principal with interest, he or she can continue to borrow against the line of credit during the agreed-upon time period. A line of credit can be unsecured or secured. Also called a credit line.

Liquidity – The ability of an asset to be converted into cash quickly.

Loan – An agreement between a borrower and a lender, where the borrower agrees to repay money with interest over a period of time.

Loan to value (LTV) – The ratio of the amount borrowed to the appraised value or sales price of real property expressed as a percentage.

Long-term care insurance – Some illnesses and injuries require specialized care over a period of time that may not be covered by traditional medical insurance. If you become debilitated due to such an ailment, this type of coverage generally allows you to pay for services such as in-home health care or assistance with daily activities, adult care and assisted living.

Long-term loan – A loan that can be paid back over a period of more than one year, usually requiring interest payments.

Market value – The current value of an asset based on what a purchaser would pay. An appraisal is sometimes used to determine market value.

Matching contributions – When an employee invests dollar(s), and that investment is matched by the employer as a type of reward or compensation.

Minimum balance – A specific amount of money required by a financial institution in order to open or maintain a particular account. In some cases, a financial institution may charge the account holder fees or even close an account if the minimum balance is not maintained.

Mortgage – A loan to finance the purchase of a home, usually with defined payments and interest rates. The homeowner gives the bank a lien, called the "mortgage", on the home, which serves as collateral for the loan.

Net income – For a business, the amount of money earned after all expenses and taxes. For an individual, total take-home pay after all deductions (taxes, social security, etc.). Also called after-tax income or net salary.

Net worth – The value of a company or individual's assets. Including cash, less total liabilities.

Non-sufficient funds – The lack of enough money in an account to pay a particular check or payment. Also known as insufficient funds. A check with insufficient funds may be returned unpaid to the person cashing it. This has a negative impact on the check writer's history of handling his or her account and may prevent the opening of future accounts.

Outstanding balance – The amount still owed on a bill, loan, or credit line.

Past due – A bill not paid by its due date is said to be past due.

Pension – An annual income paid to an employee after retirement. Payments will be based upon the employee's age at retirement, final salary, and number of years on the job.

Portfolio – A collection of investments all owned by the same person or organization. For example, a portfolio might include a variety of stocks, bonds, and mutual funds.

Principal – The total amount of money borrowed, loaned, invested, etc., not including interest or service charges.

Profit – The positive gain from an investment or a business operation after subtracting all expenses.

Rate of return – The annual rate of return is the percentage change in the value of an investment. For example, if you assume you earn a 10% annual rate of return, then you are assuming that the value of your investment has grown by that percentage.

Real property assets – Land and anything permanently affixed, including buildings, fences, trees, and minerals that have monetary value and are owned by a person or a company.

Return on investment – The income that an investment produces for an investor.

Revolving credit – A type of credit that allows an individual to borrow up to a certain amount of money, repay the money borrowed with interest when it is due, and then borrow the money again. The most popular kind of revolving credit account is the credit card.

Roth Individual Retirement Account (IRA) – An individual retirement account with non-deductible contributions, subject to certain income limits, designed to provide tax-free distributions during retirement. Contributions may be withdrawn tax-free anytime. Tax-and-penalty-free withdrawals of earnings may begin when the account has been established for at least five years, and you're 59 ½ years old, for a first-time home purchase ($10,000 lifetime limit), or in the event of disability or death. Non-qualified distributions of earnings may be subject to income tax as well as a 10% IRS penalty. Unlike Traditional IRAs, you aren't required to start taking distributions at age 70 ½.

Rule of 72 – A way to estimate the time or interest rate you would need to double your money on an investment. For example, if you have an investment that's earning 8% per year, 72 divided by 8 equals 9. This means it would take about nine years for your original investment to double.

Saving account – A bank account that allows a customer to deposit and withdraw money and earn interest on the balance.

Short sale – Allows you to sell your home and use the proceeds to pay off the mortgage if you are unable to maintain payments, even if the home's market value is less than the total amount owed.

Spending limit – The maximum amount the lender is willing to make available to the borrower according to the agreement between them. For example, if you have a credit card, the agreement will usually specify the maximum amount of money you're allowed to charge (borrow).

Statement – A monthly accounting document sent to you by your bank that lists your account balance at the beginning and end of the month, and all of the checks you wrote that your bank has processed during the month. Your statement also lists other deposits, deductions, and fees, such as service charges.

Stock – Certificate of ownership in a company.

Stock exchange – An organized in which stocks are traded by members of the exchange, such as brokers and principals.

Term – A period of time over which a loan is scheduled to be repaid. For example, a home mortgage may have a 30-year term, meaning it must be repaid within 30 years.

Traditional Individual Retirement Account (IRA) – An individual tax-deferred retirement account for employed persons. Subject to certain limits, contributions are deductible against income earned that year. Interest and profits accumulate tax-deferred until the funds are withdrawn at age 59 ½ or later. Early withdrawals are subject to a 10% penalty. Withdrawals also may be subject to income tax.

Transaction – An agreement between a buyer and seller to exchange an asset for payment. In accounting, a transaction is any event recorded in the written financial records, also called the accounting books.

Trust – A contract naming a trustee to manage the investments or property within the trust for another person or entity, the trustor, for the benefit of a named beneficiary.

Will – A legal document that specifies who has rights to your assets upon your death.

Withdrawal – to take money out of an account.

References

Felder, C. H. (Ed.). (1993). *The Original African Heritage Study Bible: King James Version.* World Publishing.

Nasdaq. (2018). *Generational wealth: Why do 70% of families lose their wealth in the 2nd generation?* Nasdaq.com. https://www.nasdaq.com/articles/generational-wealth-why-do-70-of-families-lose-their-wealth-in-the-2nd-generation

Jamrisko, M., & Kolet, I. (2013). *College costs surge 500% in U.S. since 1985: Chart of the day.* Bloomberg.com. https://www.bloomberg.com

Princeton University Library. (n.d.). *Evolution of the map of Africa.* Princeton.edu. https://library.princeton.edu

Pinkett, R., Robinson, J., & Patterson, P. (2010). *Black faces in white places: 10 game-changing strategies to achieve success and find greatness.* AMACOM.

Wood, S. (2025). *20 years of tuition costs at national universities.* U.S. News & World Report. https://www.usnews.com

About the Author

BAHIR JESSIE is an experienced financial leader in Corporate Banking, Middle-Market, Non-Profit, Residential Real Estate, Commercial Real Estate, Credit Card, Small Business, Private Banking, Wealth Management, and Private Equity. Bahir provides financial education for kids, teens, young adults, adults, entrepreneurs, seniors, and the military. He has a passion to help individuals take charge of their future by providing financial education.